Taxes and Development

The Promise of Domestic Resource Mobilization

PROJECT DIRECTOR
Daniel F. Runde

PRINCIPAL AUTHOR
Conor M. Savoy

CONTRIBUTING AUTHOR
Christina M. Perkins

A Report of the CSIS Project on U.S. Leadership in Development

December 2014

CSIS | CENTER FOR STRATEGIC & INTERNATIONAL STUDIES

ROWMAN & LITTLEFIELD
Lanham • Boulder • New York • Toronto • Plymouth, UK

About CSIS

For over 50 years, the Center for Strategic and International Studies (CSIS) has worked to develop solutions to the world's greatest policy challenges. Today, CSIS scholars are providing strategic insights and bipartisan policy solutions to help decisionmakers chart a course toward a better world.

CSIS is a nonprofit organization headquartered in Washington, D.C. The Center's 220 full-time staff and large network of affiliated scholars conduct research and analysis and develop policy initiatives that look into the future and anticipate change.

Founded at the height of the Cold War by David M. Abshire and Admiral Arleigh Burke, CSIS was dedicated to finding ways to sustain American prominence and prosperity as a force for good in the world. Since 1962, CSIS has become one of the world's preeminent international institutions focused on defense and security; regional stability; and transnational challenges ranging from energy and climate to global health and economic integration.

Former U.S. senator Sam Nunn has chaired the CSIS Board of Trustees since 1999. Former deputy secretary of defense John J. Hamre became the Center's president and chief executive officer in 2000.

CSIS does not take specific policy positions; accordingly, all views expressed herein should be understood to be solely those of the author(s).

ISBN: 978-1-4422-4047-6 (pb); 978-1-4422-4048-3 (eBook)

Center for Strategic & International Studies
1616 Rhode Island Avenue, NW
Washington, DC 20036
202-887-0200 | www.csis.org

Rowman & Littlefield
4501 Forbes Boulevard
Lanham, MD 20706
301-459-3366 | www.rowman.com

Contents

Acknowledgments

This report would not have been possible without the Chevron Corporation's generous support of the Project on U.S. Leadership in Development (USLD). This report has its foundation in a series of working groups held at CSIS in spring of 2014. We are grateful to the working group members for giving their time and offering a number of perspectives on domestic resource mobilization and related issues. The meetings were held on an off-the-record, not-for-attribution basis. Needless to say, we spoke with a wide variety of individuals who work in these areas; their insights and comments contributed immensely to our understanding of the issues.

The authors are grateful for significant research support provided by USLD interns Samuel Ha, Michael Jacobs, Julia Marvin, and Lily Wang. Over the course of the project, the authors were also ably supported by a number of CSIS research staff, including Jeremiah Magpile, Charles Rice, and Caitlin Allmaier. All contributed in some way to this report, either through research or logistical support. A number of individuals lent their wisdom in reviewing earlier drafts of this report. Steve Rozner and Tessie San Martin, in particular, provided invaluable feedback that is reflected in the final product. Finally, we are appreciative of the efforts of James Dunton, CSIS's head of publications.

Executive Summary

The ability of a state to mobilize its own resources to pay for vital social services is at the heart of a well-functioning government. As developing countries have grown wealthier over the past decade, they have seen a corresponding rise in the amount of domestic revenue available. The numbers are truly staggering: in 2012 developing and emerging economies mobilized $7.7 trillion in domestic resources. Even in sub-Saharan Africa, where the pace of change has been slower, domestic resources topped $530 billion in 2012; official development assistance in contrast totaled approximately $54 billion. Some of this is driven by the commodities boom of the past several years, but much is organic growth that has seen gross domestic product (GDP) rise. These domestic numbers, plus the rapid growth in private capital flows to the developing world, radically change the calculus of development financing.

There are large challenges to overcome in generating greater domestic resources. The capacity of most governments in developing countries remains weak from a tax administration perspective: tax avoidance is rampant, tax systems are out of date, tax collectors lack the ability to gather data, and corruption is high. Moreover, many governments lack the basic ability to manage the resources they do generate, or there is a lack of oversight on how these resources are expended. All of this argues for a greater focus on domestic resource mobilization (DRM) and public financial management by the international development community.

Rhetorically, donors have endorsed the critical role that domestic resources should play in paying for development, but allocations of donors' people, time, and money have not kept pace with this endorsement. Currently, approximately 1 percent of all official development assistance is targeted at programs aimed at improving DRM. For the United States, the world's largest donor, this ends up being approximately $35 million per year out of a total budget of over $30 billion. There is some momentum to correct this underinvestment. First, in April 2014, at the High-Level Meeting of the Global Partnership for Effective Development Cooperation, developing countries called for a doubling of official development assistance (ODA) directed toward DRM. Second, Secretary of State John Kerry recently announced that the U.S. government would shift $63 million in the U.S. President's Emergency Plan for AIDS Relief (PEPFAR) account to support DRM activities in a series of countries aimed at mobilizing $1 billion over three years.

In order to correct overall underinvestment in DRM, donors must do the following:

1. Place DRM and public financial management at the center of a renewed effort around good governance;

2. Increase commitments to DRM on a bilateral level and to multidonor trust funds or multilateral initiatives; and
3. Donors should tie the use of local systems to a corresponding commitment to improve public financial management and tax systems in order to mobilize additional domestic resources.

1 Introduction

The role that domestic revenue should play in economic development has entered the mainstream debate and development policy over the past decade.[1] One reason for this is the dramatic growth and increased prosperity in much of what is classified as the developing world. Sustained economic growth for the past 10 years has raised incomes and allowed for a corresponding increase in the amount of revenue available to national governments. Finding ways to pay for development—whether official development assistance or private sources—is an endless discussion, but one that has taken on new urgency in the wake of the global financial crisis of 2008–2009. As developing countries have grown wealthier, the role of international aid as a catalyst and not the primary funder in many (but not all) countries has forced a rethink of the role of assistance. As many traditional donors continue to deal with the aftereffects of the financial crisis, it seems clear that a significant increase in aid will not occur anytime soon. Further, even without reduced aid budgets, official development assistance (ODA) is increasingly a minority shareholder in international development. In the United States, for example, ODA accounts for less than 10 percent of financial flows to developing countries; foreign direct investment, remittances, and other private sources such as philanthropy account for the balance. But, perhaps most importantly, a country's ability to raise revenue and expend it in a transparent and accountable manner is a central aspect of good governance. As a report from the Organization for Economic Cooperation and Development (OECD) notes, "Tax is not the sole determinant of rapid development but it is one pillar of an effective state, and may also provide the basis for accountable and responsive democratic systems."[2] The rhetoric and framework for donors to increase their commitment to DRM exists, but it is now time for donors to match this by increasing resources directed toward it.

The growth and scale of domestic resources in the developing world is impressive; for example, total domestic sources of revenue grew in the 54 sub-Saharan African countries from approximately $100 billion in 2000 to nearly $530 billion in 2012.[3] Contrast that with the growth of ODA during the same period, which went from $20 billion to around $54 billion. This is a not inconsequential increase, but even with that ODA only equals

1. For example, the ONE campaign, which publishes an annual data report, has now included for the past two years (2013 and 2014) a section that specifically analyzes African government domestic spending.

2. Organization for Economic Cooperation and Development, *Governance, Taxation and Accountability: Issues and Practices* (OECD: Paris, 2008), 17, http://www.oecd.org/dac/governance-development/40210055.pdf.

3. African Development Bank, OECD, and UN Development Program, *African Economic Outlook 2014* (Paris: OECD, 2014), 65, http://www.africaneconomicoutlook.org/fileadmin/uploads/aeo/2014/PDF/E-Book_African_Economic_Outlook_2014.pdf.

approximately 11 percent of all domestic resources. To be sure, some of this growth is driven by natural resource–rich countries and the corresponding high commodity prices over the last decade or so. Yet it is also the result of a growing middle class and an increase in businesses registered in the formal sector through reforms triggered by efforts such as the World Bank's *Doing Business Report*. These domestic resources contribute nearly 70 percent of all development finance available in Africa.[4] This varies from country to country, and in low-income countries there are fewer resources overall. This is not just a phenomenon in sub-Saharan Africa either; all developing regions—Latin America, South-East Asia, and so on—have seen similar growth. More broadly, domestic resource mobilization in developing and emerging economies grew to $7.7 trillion in 2012, which represents an annual increase of 14 percent since 2000.[5]

Since the adoption of the Millennium Development Goals in 2000, how to pay for achieving these large-scale goals has been a central focus of the broader donor conversation. Early conversations largely focused on donors meeting the 0.7 percent of Gross National Income GNI commitment, though DRM gained some attention in the 2002 Monterey Consensus for Financing Development. Aid recipients later committed to "intensify efforts to mobilize domestic resources" in the 2005 Paris Declaration on Aid Effectiveness.[6] The international development community continued to highlight domestic resources in subsequent meetings in Accra and Doha in 2008, and Busan in 2011. However, for DRM, the April 2014 High-Level Meeting in Mexico City could prove to be a turning point. DRM is one of four thematic areas endorsed as part of the Global Partnership for Effective Development Cooperation, and as the communiqué from Mexico City states, "We recognize the critical challenge of ensuring the adequate mobilization of government revenues of public and private domestic resources to support development. . . . Adequate mobilization of government revenues is required for direct financing and for leveraging private funds for investments in public services and social protection, institutional and human development, basic infrastructure, and strong and inclusive economic growth."[7]

Importantly, developing countries at the High-Level Meeting endorsed the need for a greater focus on DRM, signaling a demand-driven proposition as opposed to one imposed by donors. This is important, because it is easy to look at a topic such as DRM and view it as a supply-driven proposition by donors looking to reduce their foreign aid budgets. The motivation for a developing country is clear: greater DRM strengthens a government's accountability and ability to deliver the social goods that citizens expect; it helps fulfill the social

4. OECD, "Taxation and Aid for Domestic Resource Mobilization (D.R.M.)," n.d., http://www.oecd.org/site/devaeo10/44272298.pdf.

5. World Bank, *Financing for Development Post-2015* (Washington, DC: World Bank, October 2013), 9, http://www.worldbank.org/content/dam/Worldbank/document/Poverty%20documents/WB-PREM%20financing-for-development-pub-10-11-13web.pdf.

6. OECD, "The Paris Declaration on Aid Effectiveness and the Accra Agenda for Action," 2005/2008, http://www.oecd.org/dac/effectiveness/34428351.pdf.

7. Global Partnership for Effective Development Co-operation, "First High-Level Meeting of the Global Partnership for Effective Development Co-operation: Building Towards an Inclusive Post-2015 Development Agenda," Consensus Draft of the Mexico HLM Communique, April 16, 2014, http://effectivecooperation.org/wordpress/wp-content/uploads/2014/04/ConsensusDraftoftheMexicoHLMDeclaration.pdf.

compact between citizens and government and offers countries a path to self-sufficiency. The International Monetary Fund (IMF) puts it succinctly: "An effective tax system is a core function of an effective state."[8] There are, however, clear challenges to generating greater domestic resources in developing countries. Tax bases remain small, because of the size of the informal economy, the proliferation of tax exemptions and reliefs, and there is significant distrust of how the government spends its revenue. Capacity to increase revenue is limited by the institutional and human capacity of the agencies charged with implementing taxation. How resources are expended is frequently inefficient, because of subsidies, and poor budgeting and procurement capacities. And, of course, greater revenue mobilization is challenged by corruption, tax evasion, and illicit financial flows. Ultimately, these challenges illustrate that a focus on DRM is a key building block for improved overall governance.

This is an opportune moment to deepen the conversation around DRM. The Millennium Development Goals are set to expire in 2015 and the process to determine a new set of goals to replace the original MDGs is well underway. New goals will be agreed upon at a UN conference in September 2015. Prior to that the UN has announced that the Third International Conference on Financing Development will be held in Addis Ababa in June 2015.[9] This conference will build off the two prior held in Monterrey in 2002 and Doha in 2008. As a recent piece by Molly Elgin-Cossart of the Center for American Progress points out, it is important that the international community is not only having the "what" conversation, but also the "how" conversation in terms of how to achieve the new MDGs.[10] Moreover, it is important that the "how" conversation takes place prior to the "what"; clearly, domestic resource mobilization will be at the center of the Addis Ababa conference, making it all the more important that donors are prepared to take action in support of any commitments that emerge in June 2015.

Understanding what domestic resource mobilization means as a concept is central to this discussion. DRM is typically defined as the resources, both public and private, that are available for a government to fund its operations. Domestic resources consist of government revenue that is raised through taxes, fees, rent and commission on natural resource extraction, or other kinds of levies imposed on income or goods. DRM can include building the domestic financial system in order to foster greater domestic savings that can then be used to fund investments; however, this report is primarily concerned with the revenues that are directly available to governments through taxation and other sources of revenue.

This report will examine the current landscape of development finance and where DRM fits into this new landscape, trace how DRM has emerged as a development priority and how donors tackle DRM, and finally will make a series of recommendations and conclusions.

---

8. International Monetary Fund, *Tax Policy and Administration: Securing Revenue for Development* (Washington, DC: IMF, April 2011), http://www.imf.org/external/np/otm/2010/100110.pdf.

9. United Nations, "Resolution 68/279: Modalities for the Third International Conference on Financing for Development," July 10, 2014, http://www.un.org/ga/search/view_doc.asp?symbol=A/RES/68/279&Lang=E.

10. Molly Elgin-Cossart, "Delivering Development after 2015," Center for American Progress, August 25, 2014, http://cdn.americanprogress.org/wp-content/uploads/2014/08/CossartDevelopment_brief.pdf.

2 | Sources of Development Financing

The landscape of development financing has shifted markedly in the past 15 years. Global capital flows to developing countries were once dominated by various forms of foreign aid, but are now largely composed of foreign direct investment and remittances. Assistance from the United States, for example, is responsible for 10 percent of capital flows each year; foreign direct investment, remittances, and other private sources such as philanthropy account for the balance. The immense and growing domestic resources that are available to developing countries, however, have largely been absent from the development finance conversation.

The financing needs in developing countries are immense. The OECD estimated in 2012 that a minimum of $120 billion per year was needed to meet Millennium Development Goals 1–6 (MDGs).[1] This would require approximately $62.1 billion spent in 20 low-income countries and $59.2 billion in 79 low- and middle-income countries. To alleviate extreme hunger by 2020, $50.2 billion is needed per year; to provide universal access to healthcare by 2020, $37 billion is needed per year; and to ensure universal access to primary education by 2020, $42 billion is needed per year.[2] This is to say nothing of the financing that is needed to meet the significant infrastructure needs of many of these countries. In sub-Saharan Africa, the World Bank calculated that an additional $93 billion was needed for infrastructure alone. Across the developing world, financing for infrastructure is estimated to equal $1 trillion per year until 2020. It is believed that India alone needs approximately $1 trillion to meet its infrastructure.[3] Infrastructure, of course, can be funded through a mix of public and private resources, but social goods will continue to largely fall to government resources. Last year the OECD valued total ODA at just over $130 billion; clearly, additional financial resources will be required to meet global financing demand.

Official Development Assistance

Twelve years ago, the conversation around development financing focused on how to mobilize more ODA from traditional donors and how to ensure it was spent in the best

1. OECD, "Achieving the Millennium Development Goals: More money or better policies (or both)?," 2012, http://www.oecd.org/social/poverty/50463407.pdf.
2. Oxfam, "Oxfam: Unpaid corporate tax could solve global hunger with money to spare," press release, January 31, 2013, http://www.oxfam.org.uk/media-centre/press-releases/2013/01/liberia-hlp-meeting.
3. Deloitte, "Indian Infrastructure: A Trillion Dollar Opportunity," January 2014, http://www.deloitte.com/assets/Dcom-India/Local%20Assets/Images/Thumbnails/infra/Deloitte%20Background%20Paper_27Jan_Final2.pdf.

possible way. Much of this conversation centered on how to get donors to meet the 0.7 percent of GDP directed toward aid commitment that first emerged in donor discussions in the late 1970s. From 2002 until 2008, traditional donors massively increased ODA that reversed the downward trend prevalent in the 1990s. By 2013, five OECD Development Assistance Committee (DAC) countries (Denmark, Luxembourg, Norway, Sweden, and the UK) actually achieved the 0.7 percent mark, but all OECD-DAC members increased their aid significantly between 2002 and 2008. By 2010, global ODA was estimated to stand at $130.9 billion per year, but with many countries enacting austerity or simply making cuts to their foreign aid budgets in order to meet domestic demands, numbers have largely plateaued or increased very slightly. Where increases have occurred, it has largely come from nontraditional emerging donors (i.e., South Korea, Turkey, UAE, and so on) who have begun to play a bigger role. ODA peaked in 2013 at $134 billion, but this was largely due to a significant increase by UAE to support Egypt.

This is not true in all countries; there remain a significant number of low-income countries and fragile states that are dependent on aid to furnish a significant part of their budget, either through direct budget support or indirectly through targeted project-based aid programs. In sub-Saharan Africa, there are a number of countries that continue to receive more than 25 percent of their national budget each year in the form of ODA. The evidence is mixed as far as the effect that aid dependency has on a state's willingness to mobilize domestic resources. There is a general sense that increased aid flows can reduce the pressure for a government to raise revenue, pursue reforms, or broaden the tax base, yet empirical studies are mixed.[4] Recent research by the International Centre for Tax and Development utilizing a new government revenue database, suggests that at best there is a positive relation, and at worst a neutral one.[5] Ultimately, reducing aid dependency is in both donors and recipient countries best interest in order to reduce reliance on unpredictable aid flows. It also means that regardless of whether the country is "aid dependent" or receives a smaller amount of aid each year, donors must look to focus ODA more on catalytic activities.

Domestic Revenue

The massive increase in domestic revenue—direct taxes (income, corporate, and so on), indirect taxes, natural resource revenue—is one of the most promising results of the sustained economic growth in the developing world over the past decade or so. Although lower-income countries continue to generate as a percentage of GDP a smaller amount of taxes than high-income OECD countries, the trend has been toward greater domestic revenue that can be applied to meet the development needs of countries. A recent report by the International Center for Tax and Development found that "overall tax collection exhibited a strongly upward trend in the developing world over the two decades ending in 2009/2010,

4. OECD, *Governance, Taxation and Accountability*, 19.
5. See Kyle McNabb and Philippe LeMay-Boucher, *Tax Structures, Economic Growth and Development*, Working Paper No. 22 (Brighton, UK: International Centre for Tax and Development, September 2014), http://www.ictd.ac/sites/default/files/ICTD%20WP22.pdf.

and this pattern was relatively consistent across income groups and regions."[6] This is a significant statement and one that is at the heart of why domestic resources are so critical to the financing of the post-2015 agenda.

In order to better understand the potential role and where reform is needed, it is important to look at the structure and composition of taxes in developing countries. Tax structures are generally divided into direct and indirect taxes. Direct taxes are personal income tax, corporate tax, and property taxes; indirect taxes are taxes on goods and services (value-added tax and sales tax) or trade taxes. Developing countries draw the majority of their revenue from indirect taxes relying heavily on trade taxes, though, as a percentage of total revenue, these indirect taxes have declined over the past two decades. This traditional reliance on trade taxes is largely due to the fact that it is easier for developing countries to collect trade taxes at ports and borders, as opposed to income tax.[7] As trade liberalization has increased in recent years, developing countries have generally reduced this reliance, and now trade taxes make up 20 percent of total tax revenue in lower-income countries. To replace this decline in revenue, lower-income countries have increasingly turned to taxing goods and services, largely through the introduction of value-added taxes. The trend is similar in countries classified as middle income.[8] Meanwhile, direct taxes as a percentage of total revenue collected, especially personal income tax, remain relatively low in lower- and middle-income countries holding steady at around 10–11 percent. Though, it should be noted, direct taxes as a percentage of GDP in lower-income countries have still grown from 4 percent to 6 percent during this period.[9]

In spite of this growth, tax-to-GDP ratio remains persistently low across developing regions. In low-income countries, the average ratio is in the 10 to 15 percent range, while middle-income countries do slightly better at around 20 percent, but neither meets the high-income standard of 20–30 percent. And yet, although many developing countries have not seen their tax-to-GDP ratio budge much over the past two decades, they have seen an increase in the amount of revenue available through the concurrent rise in GDP. The Philippines, for example, has seen its total government revenue climb from $10.3 billion in 2001 to $38.3 billion in 2011—although its tax-to-GDP ratio has stayed hovering between 13.5 percent and 14 percent.[10] Figures such as these are repeated in a number of developing countries across a spectrum of regions and income levels. (See Appendix 1 for charts and graphs of government revenue for a sample of 11 countries.)

6. Wilson Prichard, Alex Cobham, and Andrew Goodall, *The ICTD Government Revenue Dataset*, Working Paper No. 19 (Brighton, UK: International Centre for Tax and Development, September 2014), 36, http://www.ictd.ac/sites/default/files/ICTD%20WP19.pdf.

7. McNabb and LeMay-Boucher, *Tax Structures, Economic Growth, and Development*, 13.

8. Ibid., 16.

9. Prichard et al., *The ICTD Government Revenue Dataset*, 38.

10. IMF, "Philippines: 2014 Article IV Consultation—Staff Report," August 2014, 9, https://www.imf.org/external/pubs/ft/scr/2014/cr14245.pdf.

Sovereign Debt

At the beginning of the twenty-first century, the topic of sovereign debt in developing countries focused on the crushing debt that many had incurred since independence. This led to a movement for "debt relief" from creditors in order to reduce this burden and free up resources that could be spent on spurring economic growth. The international community went so far as to coin a term that described these countries—heavily indebted poor countries (HIPCs). Eventually the debt relief campaign convinced the G8 to forgive all debt owed to the World Bank and IMF—approximately $70 billion—by HIPCs. This was a significant step that freed up $1 billion per year that countries previously directed toward debt service payments. Steve Radelet, former USAID chief economist, cited debt relief as one of the trends that helped to propel the 17 countries he cited as "emerging" African countries.[11]

The position of many formerly HIPCs has shifted markedly since debt relief, with many now able to tap international capital markets. Further, there has been a rise in the number of investment-grade countries in developing regions. According to rating agency Fitch, this number climbed from 10 countries in 1998 to 25 in 2011.[12] To be sure, most developing countries borrow the majority of their debt from domestic sources, but with an improvement in credit ratings many are looking to diversify their debt sources. In 2000, sub-Saharan African countries issued just $1 billion in sovereign debt on the international capital market; last year this figure stood at $11 billion.[13] Beginning in 2007, a number of sub-Saharan African countries issued bonds by tapping Eurobonds, including:

Gabon in 2007: $1 billion Eurobond

Ghana in 2007: $750 million Eurobond

Senegal in 2011: $500 million Eurobond

Nigeria in 2011: $500 million Eurobond

Namibia in 2011: $500 million Eurobond

Angola in 2012: $1 billion Eurobond

Zambia in 2012: $750 million Eurobond

Rwanda in 2013: $400 million Eurobond

Tanzania in 2013: $600 million Eurobond

11. Steven Radelet, "Emerging Africa: How 17 Countries Are Leading the Way," Center for Global Development, September 2010, http://www.cgdev.org/files/1424419_file_EmergingAfrica_FINAL.pdf.

12. Fitch Credit Ratings, "Fitch—Complete Sovereign Rating History," accessed October 2014, https://www.fitchratings.com/web_content/ratings/sovereign_ratings_history.xls.

13. Katrina Manson and Javier Blas, "Kenya launches $2bn debut bond roadshow," *Financial Times*, June 4, 2014, http://www.ft.com/intl/cms/s/0/ff8b55dc-ebd0-11e3-8cef-00144feabdc0.html?siteedition=intl#axzz3AkO3jj80.

Zambia in 2014: $1 billion Eurobond

Kenya in 2014: $2 billion Eurobond

This means these nine countries have successfully tapped an additional $6 billion in funds that have largely been directed toward badly needed infrastructure projects. Moreover, these bonds have proven attractive to African governments because the interest payments are far lower than on domestic debt. Ghana's 2007 10-year Eurobond was estimated to yield around 5 percent in May 2013 as opposed to yields on domestic bonds closer to 20 percent.[14] Having access to these markets also offers African governments an alternative source of funding should other traditional sources vanish. An S&P analyst report from May 2013 notes that Rwanda issued its $400 million Eurobond following the suspension of ODA by a number of donors over concerns about President Kagame's crackdown on opposition politicians.

Although there is much to be optimistic about regarding sovereign debt as a source of funding for developing countries (and investors certainly are), there is a need to be cautious given continued weak fiscal management. This highlights that activities around DRM cannot be solely limited to improved tax administration and tax collection, but must also focus on the broader goals of good public financial management. This means a focus on budget formulation and execution, debt management, parliamentary oversight of budgets, and others. It is important to recognize that even in countries that are seen as relatively good performers, there are significant challenges that remain around how governments expend their resources.

Ghana is an example of a country that recently had a fiscal windfall but is now struggling with how to best manage its domestic resources. Over the past decade, the country has emerged as a stable democracy with increasingly strong governance and rule of law. Most importantly, oil production began in 2010 that has proved to be a fiscal windfall. In spite of some initial promising moves such as passing the Petroleum Revenue Management Act of 2011, Ghana has struggled to use the new resources in a fiscally responsible manner. Instead of deploying the resources to bolster investment in key sectors, the Ghanaian government hiked civil service salaries and increased costly fuel subsidies. After seeing its debt to GDP ratio decline and its budget deficit shrink from 24 percent of GDP in 2009 to 10 percent in 2012, both have ballooned over the past two years in order to finance the new spending. This new spending has also been paid for with an increase in domestic borrowing and two bonds floated on the international capital markets (2007 and 2013). The worsening economic situation has caused the Ghanaian cedi to depreciate by 40 percent versus the U.S. dollar, and in August 2014 the government requested IMF support to manage the fiscal crisis.[15]

---

14. Christian Esters, "The Growing Allure of Eurobonds for African Sovereigns," Standard & Poor's Ratings Services, May 6, 2013, http://www.standardandpoors.com/spf/upload/Ratings_EMEA/2013-05-06_TheGrowingAllureOfEurobonds.pdf.

15. Robert Looney, "Can Ghana's Democracy Save it from the Oil Curse," *Foreign Policy*, May 1, 2014, http://www.foreignpolicy.com/articles/2014/05/01/can_ghanas_democracy_save_it_from_the_oil_curse; Alan Beattie, "Ghana's warning to Africa," *Financial Times*, August 7, 2014, http://blogs.ft.com/beyond-brics/2014/08/07/ghanas-warning-to-africa/.

3 | DRM as a Development Priority

Traditionally, DRM has not been a donor priority; it has largely been relegated to the sidelines of the broader, technocratic governance discussion. The 2002 Monterrey Consensus on Financing for Development identified DRM as the first of six financial pillars that would meet the MDGs. Donors agreed at Monterrey to tackle DRM through the following commitments: supportive enabling environment, good governance, control of corruption, sound macroeconomic policies, public resources/budgeting, sound banking systems, microfinance/small and medium enterprise financing, and capacity building.[1] Although the communique from Monterrey clearly endorsed DRM as essential to financing development, it is unclear what long-term effect this had on spurring the reforms needed to increase domestic resources. Much of the focus from 2002 onward was on debt relief for heavily indebted developing countries and a corresponding increase in the amount of ODA available. At the same time, the donor community focused on aid effectiveness through the Paris Declaration in 2005 and subsequent meetings in Accra in 2008 and Busan in 2011. In order to achieve aid effectiveness, the donor community sought to better align their efforts with country priorities and to increase country ownership of development.

DRM played a role in the 2005 Paris Declaration on Aid Effectiveness, the 2008 Accra Agenda for Action, and 2011 Busan Agreement; however, it was relatively minor in comparison to other priorities. In some sense, this seems to be attributable to the fact that these earlier documents focused on *aid effectiveness* as opposed to *development effectiveness*. The aid effectiveness agenda was much more focused on how to make official development assistance from traditional donors more effective in achieving economic and human development. Under the Paris Declaration, donors and recipient countries committed to achieving this through five principles:

1. Ownership: Developing countries set their own strategies for poverty reduction, improve their institutions, and tackle corruption;
2. Alignment: Donor countries align behind these objectives and use local systems;
3. Harmonization: Developing countries coordinate, simplify procedures, and share information to avoid duplication;

1. U.S. State Department, "Mobilizing Domestic Financial Resources for Development," February 14, 2008, http://2001-2009.state.gov/e/eeb/rls/othr/2008/106384.htm.

4. Results: Developing countries and donors shift focus to development results and results get measured; and

5. Mutual Accountability: Donors and partners are accountable for development results.[2]

Much of this was then translated into an increased reliance on country systems through general or sector budget support by donors, ensuring that aid was released in a timely fashion, and the untying of aid. This made sense in the context of 2002–2008 as traditional donors continued to increase the amount of ODA available each year, but it made less sense post-2008 as the global financial crisis put an increased strain on foreign aid budgets.

The Busan Partnership in 2011 fundamentally shifted the donor discussion around the role of domestic resources. The document that came out of this meeting made clear that "aid is only part of the solution to development," and in order to ensure effective development, "Governments' own revenues [must] play a greater role in financing their development needs. In turn, governments are more accountable to their citizens for the development results they achieve."[3] This represented a growing recognition on the part of all engaged in development that traditional donors faced growing budgetary constraints that lead to either flat growth in ODA or, in several cases, reduction or elimination of ODA. In addition, the international development discussion post-2008 focused far more on integrating the disparate pieces of the development community and moving beyond simply a donor-to-recipient government conversation. This meant looking at the role that trade and investment flows, remittances, philanthropy, and others played in financing development. But there was also a growing recognition that by raising a country's own resources it *increased* country ownership.

The process that began in Paris is now known officially as the Global Partnership for Effective Development Cooperation, which held its first High-Level Meeting in Mexico City in April 2014. DRM is a pillar of the partnership, being seen as the primary means to fund development efforts going forward. As with earlier international efforts, the final communique from the first High-Level Meeting of the partnership underlined the critical role sufficient government and other domestic resources can play in paying for development.[4] During the meeting itself, a plenary session was held that examined effective taxation and domestic resource mobilization for development. The plenary session endorsed six steps for improved domestic resources for development:

1. Form a coalition for "sustainably resourced public service delivery";

2. Commitment by donors to increase and refine ways to measure ODA targeted at tax systems development;

---

2. OECD, "The Paris Declaration on Aid Effectiveness: Five Principles for Smart Aid," n.d., http://www.oecd.org/dac/effectiveness/45827300.pdf.

3. OECD, "Busan Partnership for Effective Development Co-operation," December 1, 2011, 9, http://www.oecd.org/dac/effectiveness/49650173.pdf.

4. Global Partnership for Effective Development Co-operation, "First High-Level Meeting of the Global Partnership for Effective Development Co-operation: Building Towards an Inclusive Post-2015 Development Agenda," Mexico High Level Meeting Communiqué, April 16, 2014, paragraphs 20–22, http://effectivecooperation.org/wordpress/wp-content/uploads/2014/07/ENG_Final-ConsensusMexicoHLMCommunique.pdf.

3. The OECD's "principles for international engagement in supporting developing countries in revenue matters";
4. The OECD's "tax inspectors without borders" as an example of innovation to address international tax avoidance;
5. The IMF-led "tax administration diagnostic assessment tool;" and
6. Commit to perform risk analyses against exposure to illicit financial flows.[5]

As with many donor interventions, there is a need for political will on the part of developing countries to make the necessary reforms. Donors must ask how one can foster political will to tackle issues around tax that are often directly tied to entrenched political and economic power bases. Technical assistance can help reform processes and train individuals, but it cannot create the will needed to sustain potential benefits. There is a seeming converging consensus given the place that DRM has in the global partnership; especially because this appears to be demand driven. The most forceful endorsement of DRM came from Nigerian finance minister Ngozi Okonjo-Iweala, who delivered the keynote address at the plenary on DRM at the April 2014 Mexico City meeting. She laid out the clear benefits for developing countries to generate significant domestic resources to pay for development and called on donors to increase the amount of ODA directed toward DRM from 1 percent per year to 2 percent.[6] Donors should not be deaf to this call to action; if the leading voice for an increased focus on DRM is the finance minister of Nigeria, they need not fear perceived repercussions. Instead, they must work with like-minded governments in developing countries to generate the political will to make the necessary and often painful reforms. Donors are not powerless to help create political will. First, they can continue to hold government-to-government policy dialogues on the need to generate additional government revenue and the need to expend this in an efficient, transparent way. This is also particularly important because of the increased push for the use of country systems under the global partnership.

Second, and perhaps more important than policy dialogues, donors should work with civil society and NGOs to help citizens hold their governments accountable. In many countries, there is deep distrust of tax systems because of corruption and a lack of transparency or effective service delivery. This lack of legitimacy contributes to the small tax bases that exist in many developing countries. People feel that the system is skewed to favor elites and that governments deliver few of the social goods they need. On the private sector side, this lack of trust and legitimacy contributes to why so many businesses remain in the informal sector.

5. OECD, "Plenary Session 2: Partnering for Effective Taxation and Domestic Resource Mobilization," April 15, 2014, http://effectivecooperation.org/wordpress/wp-content/uploads/2014/04/Plenary-Session-2-DRM.pdf.
6. Ngozi Okonjo-Iweala, "Partnering for Effective Taxation and Domestic Resource Mobilisation for Development" (speech, First High-Level Meeting, Mexico City, April 2014), http://effectivecooperation.org/2533-2/.

4 | Challenges and Opportunities for DRM

In spite of the growth in domestic revenue in developing countries, significant challenges remain both in terms of generating additional revenue and in ensuring that revenue is expended in a responsible manner. Unlike high-income countries, developing countries typically depend on import duties, natural resources, and taxes paid by companies to provide the majority of government revenues.[1] Personal income tax remains largely untapped given the size and persistence of the informal sector. From a tax and revenue administration perspective, the challenges that continue to affect developing countries mobilizing greater domestic resources can be grouped into four broad categories:

1. Limited taxation capacity;
2. Unsustainable natural resource revenue;
3. Inefficient allocation and expenditure of resources; and
4. Illicit financial flows.

This report is primarily concerned with the first three areas, but a quick note on illicit financial flows. Illicit financial flows from developing countries remain a persistent and large issue affecting the effective mobilization of domestic resources. This involves corruption, transfer pricing issues, and other illicit flows. This is a large and growing problem, but is best left for a separate study.

- *Taxation capacity.* The capacity of developing countries to tax remains relatively low. This manifests itself through a small tax base, insignificant tax administration capacity, and extensive loopholes that allow revenue to go untapped. In Ghana, for example, tax incentives offered to foreign companies cost them approximately 2 to 3 percent in lost revenue every year. This is equal to approximately $1.2 billion or the equivalence of the entire public health budget of the country for 2014.

  A principle issue for developing countries that reduces revenue available for development purposes is the limited size of the tax base, which has kept the

1. Mick Moore, "The Changing Politics of Tax Policy Reform in Developing Countries," PREM Notes, February 2013, http://siteresources.worldbank.org/PUBLICSECTORANDGOVERNANCE/Resources/285741-1361973400317/GPSM2_v2.pdf.

overall tax-to-GDP ratio in most developing countries relatively low even as these countries have seen revenues rise driven by overall economic growth. In lower-income countries, the tax-to-GDP ratio is typically in the 10–14 percent range, whereas high-income countries generate more in the 20–30 percent range. The tax base in developing countries is limited for several reasons, but the most important is the size and persistence of the informal sector. This leads to a dependence on a narrow base of taxpayers—either individual or corporate—and other types of tax such as value-added tax (VAT). A 2009 USAID diagnostic found that in Kenya, for example, an estimated 75 percent of all domestic taxes and 40 percent of total taxes are paid by just 830 individuals.[2] Beyond issues of informality, the narrow base of taxpayers exists because of concern over corruption and misuse of government revenue, burdensome and time-consuming tax compliance procedures, and the proliferation of tax emptions, holidays, and other tax reliefs that further erode the tax base.

Tax administration remains a significant stumbling block for many countries in the developing world due to a combination of poor policies and weak administrative capacity. In countries that lack natural resources and have generated higher domestic revenue, the key has been a "well-functioning and implementable tax system with an efficient tax administration."[3] But for many countries, the institutional and human capacity remains low, systems and procedures are outdated or complex, the legal and fiscal framework is unclear, and there is a lack of coordination among relevant agencies and offices.

Capacity is further weakened by the extensive loopholes that exist both in tax codes and outside the tax code, and by the widespread evasion of taxes that occurs. Largely this is due to the bargaining power that a variety of vested interests—companies, wealthy individuals, and others—have in countries with limited tax bases. The limited size of the tax base and the need for revenue gives significant power to these groups, who can then use it to gain exceptions or loopholes that are beneficial to them. This results in frequent policy changes as governments engage in small changes to the tax code, which further weakens the capacity of governments to raise revenue and reduces the likelihood that ordinary citizens will feel compelled to pay taxes.[4]

- *Management of natural resources revenue.* For some developing countries, revenue from natural resources such as oil and gas or minerals has contributed to the growth in domestic resources available, offering a cash windfall to previously strapped governments. Yet this is a double-edged sword, with the increase in revenue creating a "resource curse" where the mismanagement of these newfound resources leads to

2. U.S. Agency for International Development (USAID), *Kenya's Agenda for Action: Commercial Legal and Institutional Reform Diagnostic of Kenya's Business Environment* (Washington, DC: USAID, June 2009), 92, http://egateg.usaid.gov/sites/default/files/Kenya.pdf.

3. Roy Culpeper and Aniket Bhushan, "Domestic Resource Mobilization: A Neglected Factor in Development Strategy," North-South Institute, April 2008, http://www.bookiejar.com/Content/Books/00a4f3e0-2dfa-4573-9b16-039253b9b61e/207_r1/OEBPS/chapter_0001.html.

4. Moore, "The Changing Politics of Tax Policy Reform in Development Countries."

greater trouble. As the *Financial Times* once summed it up, "From the civil war battlefields of southern Sudan to the slums of Angola and the swamps of the Niger Delta, the discovery of crude has done little to improve local lives. Often, it has destroyed them."[5] This dependency on natural resources reduces a government's incentive to be accountable, efficient, or responsive to the needs of its citizens. In addition, revenue derived from natural resources is subject to the inherent instability of international commodity markets; certainly, in recent years there has been a boom in commodity prices and this has benefited developing countries, but as supplies have increase, prices are predictably falling. The numbers of dependency are staggering. In sub-Saharan Africa, 20 countries are dependent on natural resources for 30 percent or more of their exports; this translates into nine countries that are then dependent on revenue from natural resources for 20 percent or more of their annual government budget. Proper management of the revenue from natural resource extraction is critical for resource-rich countries and must be a component of the DRM discussion. Bilateral donors, such as Norway or the United States, who have managed their own rich natural resources, should help to provide alternative models of how to manage the wealth that stems from these resources.

- *Efficiency of expenditures.* Increased domestic revenues have triggered a corresponding increase in government expenditures in most, if not all, countries. In many cases, government expenditures remain extremely inefficient for three primary reasons: 1) unsustainable subsidies that crowd out investment in other sectors; 2) inefficient government procurement processes; and 3) rapid accumulation of new government debt, such as in Ghana, where interest payments at increasingly high interest rates are squeezing capital investments and other productive spending. This has been a particular issue in countries that have seen a windfall through the development of new natural resources or because of high commodity prices over the past decade. Moreover, this demonstrates the need for donors to focus on more than just reform of DRM and include it as part of broader public financial management reform.

Subsidies, in particular, are a major challenge to the efficiency of developing countries' management of financial resources, as they represent a source of revenue that is often misdirected in order to either artificially control a market or maintain political support. Worldwide, it is estimated that the cost of all subsidies equals $1.9 trillion or 8 percent of total government spending; energy subsidies alone equal $480 billion. On a country level, the impact of subsidies is even starker. In Indonesia, for example, the government spent over 300 trillion rupiah in 2012 on energy subsides (largely for petrol) that equaled 20 percent of all government spending that year. Put another way, Indonesia's energy subsidy was double the fiscal deficit of 153 trillion rupiah.[6] Subsidies, especially on the energy side, are politically popular, and leaders

5. Matthew Green, "Crude Realities," *Financial Times*, August 27, 2008, http://www.ft.com/intl/cms/s/0/031d2aea-7459-11dd-bc91-0000779fd18c.html#axzz3GnIGMd8r.
6. IMF, "Indonesia: Staff Report for the 2013 Article IV Consultation," December 2013, http://www.imf.org/external/pubs/ft/scr/2013/cr13362.pdf.

frequently argue that they are intended to benefit the poor. However, evidence suggests this is not the case, with recent research in sub-Saharan Africa showing that energy and fuel subsidies were skewed toward higher-income households. This is not surprising, since these individuals have better access to electricity and are more likely to own an auto.[7]

Government procurement practices remain extremely weak in most developing countries, and this causes significant inefficiencies in the government expenditure process. Transparency International estimates that corruption in the procurement process can add up to 20–25 percent to costs; the Asian Development Bank estimates that governments in developing Asia have overpaid anywhere from 20 to 100 percent more for goods and services than they would otherwise.

Donor Efforts

DRM remains a low priority for most donors in spite of the increase in rhetoric. This is reflected in the amount of ODA that is directed toward DRM, which in 2011 was estimated to be $104.6 million or less than 0.07 percent of total global ODA that year. That same year, donors spent an additional $579 million on projects that had "an identifiable DRM component."[8] The 2011 number does represent an increase from 2006, when donors spent approximately 0.04 percent of total ODA on DRM projects. In 2011, donors disbursed money to 75 countries, with the top recipients being Afghanistan ($17.8 million) and Pakistan (approximately $17 million). These numbers help to illustrate the fact that in spite of the rhetoric surrounding the important role DRM must play in financing development, donors still have a long way to go in terms of support. Yet, in spite of the low funding available, there have been some effective efforts over the past several years aimed at increasing domestic resources.

The IMF has taken a leading role in designing and sponsoring tax reform efforts through a variety of technical assistance (TA) missions that target lower-income countries, in particular those in sub-Saharan Africa (currently 31 TA missions underway). The IMF tackles this through a number of measures, but their most prominent is a Topical Trust Fund that was established in 2011 and is designed to provide technical assistance missions to low- and lower middle–income countries to help implement reforms. The Tax Policy and Administration trust fund is scheduled to run for five years at a cost of approximately $30 million.[9] This trust fund builds on the IMF's decades of technical assistance work. On a basic level, this assistance has included preparation for adoption of VAT, creation of large taxpayer offices, and registration systems. More broadly, the IMF has worked to help

---

7. IMF, *Regional Economic Outlook: Sub-Saharan Africa, Building Momentum in a Multi-Speed World* (Washington, DC: IMF, May 2013), 50, https://www.imf.org/external/pubs/ft/reo/2013/afr/eng/sreo0513.pdf.

8. Tim Swanson and Guto Ifan, "Aid for domestic resource mobilisation: how much is there?," Development Initiatives, February 2014, 3–4, http://devinit.org/wp-content/uploads/2014/02/Aid-for-domestic-resource-mobilisation-%E2%80%93-how-much-is-there.pdf.

9. IMF, *Tax Policy and Administration*, 4.

implement modernization strategies and introduce risk management, audit services, and performance assessment systems.[10]

In its work in sub-Saharan Africa, the IMF has seen some significant progress. Since 1995, working in concert with the French government, the IMF has pursued an aggressive tax reform effort in 19 Francophone African countries.[11] These reforms have focused on fostering tax compliance; reducing taxpayers' compliance costs; improving taxpayer services; reducing tax administration's costs; increasing transparency and strengthening integrity; developing risk management and combating tax fraud; and strengthening collection enforcement.[12] These reforms resulted in most cases in the merging of the tax administration's functions into a unified tax office, the introduction of risk management, and improved tax administration through a streamlining of processes. The results for revenue mobilization were impressive, with all but three of the 19 countries seeing double-digit increases in tax revenue as a proportion of GDP between 1995 and 2012.

In addition to the IMF, the OECD has taken a lead role in developing policy and raising awareness of the role that DRM can play in development. Through its Tax and Development initiative, the OECD has helped to craft much of the policy that justifies the inclusion of DRM in the Global Partnership. The OECD launched its Tax and Development initiative in January 2010 following a meeting between the Committee on Fiscal Affairs and the DAC. Subsequently the OECD's task force has focused on four issue areas: state building, taxation, and aid; effective transfer pricing; increased transparency in the reporting of relevant financial data by multinational entities; and supporting the work of the global forum on transparency and exchange on information. The OECD's efforts around tax and development have generated a tremendous amount of the policy analysis that underpins the recent shift toward the importance of DRM. Importantly, the OECD (along with the UNDP) is performing the secretariat function for the Global Partnership, which will allow this policy work to support it.

Beyond the OECD's policy work, it has also recently launched the "Tax Inspectors without Borders" (TIWB) program, which was endorsed at the High-Level Meeting in Mexico City in April 2014 by the Global Partnership. TIWB was originally proposed by the OECD's Task Force on Tax and Development in July 2012 and seeks to deploy experienced tax inspectors to developing countries on a demand-driven basis to share expertise and experience. TIWB is currently in a "trial operational phase" as part of its initial 18-month mandate, which will end in December 2014. Subject to the results of this phase, the project will launch in early 2015.[13] TIWB aims to assist developing countries with increasing voluntary compliance, greater certainty and consistency for business, enhancing state-society relations,

10. Patrick Fossat and Michel Bua, *Tax Administration Reform in the Francophone Countries of Sub-Saharan Africa* (Washington, DC: IMF, July 2013), 10, http://www.imf.org/external/pubs/ft/wp/2013/wp13173.pdf.

11. The countries covered by this work are Benin, Burkina Faso, Burundi, Cameroun, Central African Republic, Chad, Comoros, Republic of Congo, Cote d'Ivoire, Djibouti, the Democratic Republic of Congo, Gabon, Guinea, Madagascar, Mali, Mauritania, Niger, Senegal, and Togo.

12. Fossat and Bua, *Tax Administration Reform in the Francophone Countries of Sub-Saharan Africa*, 15.

13. OECD, "Global Relations in Taxation: Tax Inspectors Without Borders," 2014, http://www.oecd.org/ctp/tax-global/tax-inspectors.htm.

and fostering an international dialogue on tax matters.[14] In conducting the feasibility study, the OECD found that "there is a high level of demand among tax administrations in developing countries for in-depth, practical audit assistance from expert peers."[15]

There are seven modalities through which donors can target reform of a country's tax system: general budget support, sector budget support, basket financing, other multidonor instruments, bilateral projects or programs, and funding through South-South organizations.[16] To tackle DRM, there are four key elements to produce an efficient tax system: 1) the legal and fiscal framework; 2) systems and procedures; 3) institutional and human capacity; and 4) coordination among agencies. Bilateral and multilateral agencies have pursued a multitude of different technical assistance projects in order to tackle these concerns, including tax policy, tax administration strategy, legal drafting, tax administration implementation, training and knowledge management, judicial reform, and private sector development.[17]

Current U.S. DRM Programs

USAID estimates that the United States is currently spending approximately $35 million per year on DRM-related programs. On a multiyear level, this works out to approximately $100 million to support revenue collection programs. Although this is not a high dollar amount, USAID and other U.S. development entities have pursued a number of DRM-related programs in recent years. This includes significant work in Latin America and the Caribbean, Georgia, Jordan, and the Philippines. In the Philippines, specifically, the MCC and USAID are both pursuing projects aimed at enhancing the country's ability to raise domestic resources. The MCC has a robust $54.3 million five-year program to help reform the government's revenue administration. MCC is working in partnership with the Philippines' Bureau of Internal Revenue (BIR) and the Department of Finance-Revenue Integrity Protection Service around the following activities:

- Enhancement of the electronic taxpayer information system;
- Advisory services and TA in partnership with the IMF to help the BIR with VAT audit, arrears management, and a tax gap study;
- TA collaboration with the U.S. Treasury Department's Office of Technical Assistance to help establish data-processing divisions for BIR in all of its regional offices, as well as help in redesigning tax forms;

---

14. OECD Task Force on Tax and Development, *Final Report on the Feasibility Study into the Tax Inspectors Without Borders Initiative* (Paris: OECD, June 2013), 6, http://www.oecd.org/ctp/tax-global/TIWB_feasibility_study.pdf.

15. Ibid., 8.

16. Ben Dickinson and Kjetil Hansen, *Tax and Development: Aid Modalities for Strengthening Tax Systems* (Paris: OECD-DAC, August 2012), 14–15, http://www.oecd.org/officialdocuments/publicdisplaydocumentpdf/?cote=DCD/DAC%282012%2934&docLanguage=En.

17. Geerten Michielse and Victor Thuronyi, "Overview of Cooperation on Capacity Building in Taxation," UN Committee of Experts on International Cooperation in Tax Matters, October 11, 2010, 22, http://www.un.org/esa/ffd/tax/sixthsession/OverviewCapacityBldg.pdf.

- Training and support for BIR personnel to improve investigative capacity for internal misconduct; and
- Audit support to the BIR through the utilization of automated tools.[18]

Outside of the MCC compact project, USAID in the Philippines is pursuing a $13 million project under the Partnership for Growth (PFG) that began in late 2013 to "enhance activities designed to relieve the fiscal space constraint to growth." In order to do so, USAID and the Philippines' Department of Finance are pursuing the following:

- Establishing an independent analytic unit to help set realistic national revenue targets;
- Improving coordination among different government agencies to improve tax administration;
- Updating assessments of existing fiscal incentives and the VAT, personal and corporate income tax, excise, and mining tax;
- Building institutional capacity at the BIR to "enhance reengineered tax administration"; and
- Reinvigorating the privatization program to support "the public sector's fiscal rationalization plan."[19]

Finding additional support within the U.S. assistance budget to pay for DRM will prove to be difficult given the number of existing earmarks and the lack of an identifiable political constituency to press for additional DRM spending. Many of these earmarks exist around programs or projects that are directed toward the provision of basic social services, such as public health, basic education, water, and so on. It should be noted that the countries listed above, in which the United States currently or previously pursued tax reform efforts, are ones where the budget has not been earmarked, meaning there is more flexibility available to the USAID mission director or others to reprogram existing funds to support a new project focus. Importantly, there does appear to be a shift in American thinking, with John Kerry, the secretary of state, recently announcing that $63.5 million of PEPFAR money would be shifted toward supporting DRM in Kenya, Tanzania, Zambia, Nigeria, and Vietnam. The goal is to help raise additional country resources to pay for public health–related activities; specifically, this new program hopes to raise $1 billion over three years in the countries in question.[20] ODA directed toward these activities has traditionally provided a significant percentage of the funds needed to deliver these services. Secretary Kerry's announcement is an encouraging sign that donors recognize that in order to shift this burden toward the developing countries, they must support the reforms and training needed to allow for proper resource mobilization.

---

18. Information on the Millennium Challenge Corporation (MCC) Philippines compact provided to author by USAID, July 2014.

19. Information on USAID's "Facilitating Public Investment" project in the Philippines provided to the author by USAID, July 2014.

20. John F. Kerry, "Remarks at the 2014 Frontiers in Development Conference," Washington, DC, September 19, 2014, http://www.state.gov/secretary/remarks/2014/09/231864.htm.

5 | DRM Case Studies

Zambia

Though Zambia's tax revenue as a percentage of GDP remains relatively high for sub-Saharan Africa at around 19 percent, the nation still struggles with issues that hinder potential revenue collection, particularly surrounding its copper mining industry and vast informal sector. Zambia's policies toward income and extractive taxes changed significantly from the 1990s to today, but revenue as a percentage of GDP has remained largely stable. In 2014, tax revenue amounted to 19.3% of Zambia's total GDP, and grant revenue was 0.8% of GDP. From 2004 to 2008, Zambia's dependence on foreign assistance declined significantly. ODA made up an average of 53 percent of Zambia's national budget in 2004. In 2008, this number had dropped to around 28 percent.[1] Today, the Zambian government claims that less than 5 percent of its budget comes from foreign assistance. In spite of these positive changes, many believe Zambia is still "leaving money on the table" in terms of revenue potential.

Zambia ranks as 37 out of 183 ranked countries in terms of the ease of paying taxes,[2] and has benefited from longstanding support in the tax sector from a number of actors, with the United Kingdom's Department for International Development providing the most assistance. The multi-donor Public Expenditure Management and Financial Accountability program, supported by the International Development Association, Norway, the Netherlands, Germany, Sweden, European Commission, Finland, Ireland, Denmark, and the United Kingdom, provided over USD $73 million to Zambia from 2005 to 2013.[3] The program covered 18 focus areas, including tax administration and budget preparation and execution. A large portion of the program focused on improving the institutional capacity of the Zambia Revenue Authority (ZRA), in addition to improving physical and IT infrastructure.

COPPER MINING IN ZAMBIA

Sources of tax revenue in Zambia are diverse, but the copper sector remains a significant contributor.Zambia has historically relied on the copper sector for revenue, but mining tax exemptions and other policies viewed as favorable only to mining companies have spurred

1. Odd-Helge Fjeldstad and Kari Heggstad, *The tax systems in Mozambique, Tanzania and Zambia: Capacity and constraints* (Bergen, Norway: Chr. Michelsen Institute, 2011), http://www.cmi.no/publications/file/4045-taxation-mozambique-tanzania-zambia.pdf.
2. Ibid.
3. "Cooperating partners pump US$74m into PEMFA," *The Lusaka Times*, July 11, 2008, http://www.lusakatimes.com/2008/07/11/cooperating-partners-pump-us74m-into-pemfa/.

domestic debate and unrest in the past decade. Over a third of Zambia's GDP comes from industry, with a significant measure coming from copper mining alone. From 1969 to 2000, Zambian mines were state-owned,[4] but the nation privatized its copper industry as losses in 1998 reached a high of 9 percent of GDP. Given this severe strain, the government was unable to cover operational costs or invest in the necessary projects for continued expansion. Due to this crisis and a global downward trend in copper prices, Zambia lost much of its "bargaining power" and facilitated a favorable environment for corporations willing to step in. Initial privatization agreements (development agreements) favored mining companies, but were later broken by the government as citizens demanded to see more social programs and benefits result from mining revenues.

With the goal of stabilizing the investment climate while ensuring government stakes in projects, Zambia explored four tax regimes from 2003 to 2012. While profit-based taxes may be most likely to please both parties, revenue-based taxes are much easier to calculate and administer.

Around 2004, the Zambian government incrementally regained its footing due to increasing copper prices and the high degree of sunk costs that corporations initially invested when beginning operations in Zambia. As a result, tax revenue grew fairly consistently from 2005 to present. The majority of Zambians, however, remained unsatisfied with the benefits from increased copper prices, leading to large-scale protests. Since agreements between the government and corporations remained private, citizens were unable to verify the claims of either party, further fueling dissatisfaction among Zambians. The few documents that were leaked indicated corporations were reaping significant benefits, thus further weakening the social contract between Zambians and their government.[5] In 2011, the Movement for Multi-Party Democracy lost the presidency for the first time in 20 years, which many credit to its unpopular management of extractive revenues.

As of 2011, Zambia's royalty rate on copper remained globally competitive at 6 percent, as compared to British Columbia's 15 percent or Russia's 8 percent.[6] Unfortunately, Zambia still struggles to maintain investment levels, as many investors do not believe that overall mining productivity is improving. Additionally, reforms that began in 2008 remain unresolved today. Many still believe that copper mining companies are undertaxed and that Zambia would benefit from implementing a capital gains tax or other methods to ensure more government revenue. Given the significant presence of international mining companies in Zambia, it could be beneficial for the nation to follow the example of Mozambique, whose government, in 2012, began imposing a capital gains tax on gains realized by international companies within Mozambique borders. This approach was implemented in order

4. David Manley, *Caught in a Trap: Zambia's Mineral Tax Reforms* (Brighton, UK: International Centre for Tax and Development, September 2012), http://www.ictd.ac/sites/default/files/ICTD%20Working%20Paper%205.pdf.

5. Ibid.

6. Robert F. Conrad, "Mineral Taxation in Zambia," in *Zambia: Building Prosperity from Resource Wealth*, ed. Christopher S. Adam et al. (Oxford: Oxford University Press, 2014), 84.

to increase Mozambique's attractiveness for foreign direct investment—because resource exploration and production are inherently risky activities, the government concluded that it would not be just to further increase royalties. The capital gains tax regime offered the government a novel way to increase revenues while maintaining a positive image for international investors. In 2012, the Mozambique government received almost AUS$72 million in capital gains tax from the Australian Talbot Group alone.[7]

INFORMAL SECTOR AND INCOME TAX COMPLIANCE

As part of its series of reforms, Zambia implemented income tax self-assessment in 1992,[8] prior to most other low-income countries. Self-assessment systems are less labor-intensive and more cost efficient, as the responsibility to comply is placed firmly on the taxpayer. Though Zambia did not experience increased yields following these reforms, this is largely blamed on shifting commodity prices, rather than the self-assessment policy.

From 2007 to 2009 the personal income tax generated more revenue than the VAT, which was out of the ordinary among neighboring countries. Although the tax rate of the VAT in Zambia is amongst the highest of the region at 17.5 percent (compared to 10 percent in Botswana, 12 percent in Mauritius, and 14 percent in Lesotho, South Africa, and Swaziland),[9] it is in fact the personal income tax that is of particular importance to the nation, ranging in rates from 25 percent to 35 percent.[10] One of the primary reasons for this comparatively high income tax rate can be attributed to the noncompliance of employers in Zambia to register their employees and to remit taxes to the relevant authorities.[11] Additionally, the lack of tax on capital gains means that capital income, which is primarily earned by relatively wealthy individuals, escapes taxation altogether. Hypothetically, if the compliance rate were higher and if a capital gains tax were in effect, the government would be able to obtain the same amount of revenue with much lower income tax rates, which would be in the best interest of the Zambian people.

Unfortunately, Zambia still struggles to incorporate many business actors and workers in the informal sector into the formal economy and tax base. A World Bank study estimates that 49.8% of official GDP annually comes from the informal sector, which is high even among other countries in sub-Saharan Africa (see Table 2).[12] Though there are strategies to crowd individuals into the formal sector and increase tax participation, taxing the informal sector tends to be inefficient and yield small outcomes, as the tax potential is spread

---

7. John Skoulding, "Capital Gains Tax—The New Resource Nationalism?," Oil Council, 2014, http://www.oilcouncil.com/expert_insight_articles/capital-gains-tax-new-resource-nationalism.
8. Andrew Okello, *Managing Income Tax Compliance through Self-Assessment* (Washington, DC: IMF, March 2014), http://www.imf.org/external/pubs/ft/wp/2014/wp1441.pdf.
9. Graham Glenday, *Assessment of the Current State of VAT Implementation in SADC Member States* (Durham, NC: Duke Center for International Development, August 15, 2004), https://fds.duke.edu/db/attachment/829.
10. Fjeldstad and Heggstad, *The tax systems in Mozambique, Tanzania and Zambia.*
11. Ibid.
12. Friedrich Schneider et al., *Shadow Economies All over the World: New Estimates for 162 Countries from 1999 to 2007* (Washington, DC: World Bank, July 2010), https://openknowledge.worldbank.org/bitstream/handle/10986/3928/WPS5356.pdf?sequence=1.

Table 1. Estimated Contribution of Informal Sector to GDP (average of 1999–2006)

Country	*Estimated percent contribution*	*Country*	*Estimated percent contribution*
Mauritius	22.9	Burkina Faso	41.2
South Africa	28.1	Swaziland	41.6
Namibia	30.5	Malawi	41.6
Lesotho	30.8	Mali	41.7
Cameroon	32.9	Guinea	42.2
Botswana	33.3	Ghana	42.3
Sudan	34.1	Cote d'Ivoire	43.3
Kenya	34.5	Uganda	43.3
Togo	35.2	Sierra Leone	43.3
Mauritania	35.6	Chad	44.5
Cape Verde	36.2	Senegal	44.8
Burundi	39.2	Central African Rep.	46.0
Ethiopia	39.6	Congo, Rep.	48.0
Mozambique	40.2	Congo, Dem. Rep.	48.0
Rwanda	40.2	Benin	49.6
Madagascar	40.6	Zambia	49.8
Niger	40.7	Tanzania	56.9

over so many individuals who yield relatively small incomes.[13] In 2010, Zambia had only 0.099 tax staff per population, compared to the world average of 0.82, rendering the Zambia Revenue Authority incapable of the increased personnel necessary to improve tax participation among informal actors. That being said, Zambia still benefits from a larger tax staff than the majority of sub-Saharan Africa, which averages 0.037.[14]

The percentage of total tax collection generated by the informal sector has increased from 0.27 percent in 2004 to 1.79 percent in 2009 due to the introduction of new taxes. Still, reform efforts should be focused on streamlining policies and creating incentives for businesses to formalize, rather than on tax compliance. Small and medium-sized enterprises (SMEs) must have proper incentives in order to formalize, and the Zambian government would be more likely to achieve measurable increases in revenue if they focused on crowding actors into the private sector, rather than on taxing informality. Aside from issues with the informal sector, many legally incorporated employers also fail to report their employees' earnings.[15]

Zambia ranks well on the World Bank's Doing Business indicators, but the large informal sector suggests there is an implementation gap between written policies and observed

13. Sydney Chauwa Phiri and Pamela Nakamba-Kabaso, *Taxation of the informal sector in Zambia* (Lusaka: Zambia Institute for Policy Analysis & Research, January 2012), http://www.zipar.org.zm/documents/Taxation%20of%20the%20informal%20Sector%20in%20Zambia.pdf.

14. Fjeldstad and Heggstad, *The tax systems in Mozambique, Tanzania and Zambia.*

15. Ibid.

outcomes. Still, Zambia is ranked 83 in ease of doing business and ranked 45 in terms of starting a business out of 189 countries measured. Unfortunately, Zambia also is estimated to have extremely high levels of illicit flows leaving the country.

In spite of these challenges, Zambia has great incentive to see through current and future tax reforms. Expanding the tax base will also improve governance and government accountability, as paying citizens are more likely to call for transparency and efficiency in tax administration and overall government activities. Zambia has significant challenges ahead in order to mobilize a steady tax base, but reforms already underway are headed in a positive direction. As citizens and the international community demand value for their money and increased accountability, governments will be forced to deliver in terms of revenue and expenditure management.

Senegal

As a lower middle–income country, Senegal has a growing private sector and shows signs of increasing prosperity. Senegal has experienced relative economic stability since 1994, when the 14 countries of the *Communauté financière d'Afrique* (CFA) franc zone devalued their currency in order to allow the region's products to be globally competitive.[16] In 2012, 45.25 percent of Senegal's government expenditures came from ODA, down from about 72 percent in 2000.[17] In comparison to other West African countries, Senegal has a relatively high percentage of revenue mobilization as a percentage of GDP, averaging 20 percent in recent years.

Since 1995, Senegal has received technical assistance on tax administration issues from the African Development Bank, the European Union, France, Japan, the Tax Policy and Administration Topical Trust Fund (TPA-TTF), and the World Bank, among others.[18] With more aggressive tax policy reform focusing on businesses, particularly SMEs, and a close watch on the nation's deficit, Senegal is a strong example of responsible financial management in West Africa. From 2008 to 2012, Senegal focused on tax simplification in order to ease the difficulty of paying taxes for both businesses and individuals.[19] In 2012, the IMF recommended Senegal focus on ensuring fiscal responsibility, improving public spending efficiency, improving public infrastructure, and focusing on inclusive growth. Senegal's deficit in 2013 stood at 5.5 percent of GDP, and authorities aim to reduce this to 5.1 percent of GDP in 2014.[20]

16. IMF, "Background Information: The CFA franc zone," accessed October 2014, https://www.imf.org/external/pubs/ft/fabric/backgrnd.htm#two.
17. World Bank, "World Development Indicators," last updated September 24, 2014, http://data.worldbank.org/data-catalog/world-development-indicators.
18. Fossat and Bua, *Tax Administration Reform in the Francophone Countries of Sub-Saharan Africa*, 9.
19. USAID, *AgCLIR: Senegal: Commercial Legal and Institutional Reform* (Washington, DC: USAID, September 2009), http://egateg.usaid.gov/sites/default/files/Senegal.pdf.
20. IMF, "Senegal Seventh Review Under the Policy Support Instrument and Request for Modification of Assessment Criteria—Staff Report; and Press Release," July 2014, 2, https://www.imf.org/external/pubs/ft/scr/2014/cr14177.pdf.

Earlier this year, the Senegalese government announced the launch of a new development and growth strategy. This strategy, known as the "Senegal Emerging" Plan (PSE), aims to accelerate the country's economic growth to at least 7% by 2018 and help the nation achieve a "middle-income country" status by 2035. The plan is composed of three strategic pillars:

1. Structural economic change and growth,
2. Human capital, social protection, and sustainable growth, and
3. Governance, institutions, and peace and security.

The plan will cost an estimated $21 billion, and pillar 1 alone is estimated to utilize approximately 66.5 percent of the plan's budget.[21] Within pillar 1 is the strengthening of infrastructure, and services related to transportation and energy top the agenda, with a focus on sustainable urbanization complementing infrastructural reform. The planned development and construction of 300,000 social housing units is meant to increase urban employment as well as meet the growing need expressed by rural and perirural migrants arriving in city centers like Dakar. Another area of particular focus is agricultural and aquacultural development, intended to increase community and regional food security while diminishing Senegal's dependence on food imports. Pillar 1 also indicates Senegalese interest in further developing the mineral resources sector, another step toward resource independence. The country hopes to boost trade, traffic, and tourism by establishing itself as a port of entry for all of West Africa and establishing Dakar as a regional hub for advanced services (business, health, education, entertainment, etc.).

Approximately 26% of the PSE's budget has been allocated to pillar 2, which focuses on improvements in social services and overall quality of life for Senegalese citizens. Of paramount importance is improving access to and the quality of education; this involves extending the length of the education cycle to 10 years, up from an average of 6 years,[22] as well as improving the quality of public school curriculums and instructors. Health and nutrition is another area of focus, with a particular emphasis on promoting hygienic practices and improving nutritional understanding across the country. Complementing hygienic education, pillar 2 also focuses on increased access to clean water in urban and rural areas. Improvements to social protection are outlined for the Senegalese labor force, both active and retired, as well as for members of the informal sector and other vulnerable groups. Additionally, pillar 2 outlines a broad-based focus on sustainable development, with calls for improved disaster risk management, gender equality, environmental protection, and natural resource management.

Pillar 3 will receive approximately 7.5% of PSE funding and will focus on consolidating peace and security measures as well as reinforcing social cohesion. Improving the quality

---

21. John Irish and Hugh Lawson, "Investors pledge $7.8 billion to kick-start Senegal growth plans," Reuters, February 25, 2014, http://www.reuters.com/article/2014/02/25/us-senegal-investment-idUSBREA1O0A020140225.
22. UNESCO, "World Data on Education: Senegal," 7th edition, November 2010, http://www.ibe.unesco.org/en/services/online-materials/world-data-on-education/seventh-edition-2010-11.html.

and efficiency of human rights, state rights, and social justice will be the priorities in this domain.

Improved management of public finances, strengthened anti-corruption measures, and increased governmental transparency are objectives that lay at the foundation of the "Senegal Emerging" plan (PSE).[23] The PSE receives financing primarily from three sources:

1. The government of Senegal (43.4%),
2. Technical and financial partners, such as the World Bank, IMF, and so on (40.4%), and,
3. Members of the private sector (both international and domestic) via private-public partnerships (16.3%).[24]

This ambitious plan aims to increase human development standards via improved access to services while maintaining tight expenditure goals. Officials must be particularly careful to not overestimate expected revenues, as occurred in 2013 when revenue was 1.5 percent of GDP lower than expected, partially due to large tax arrears by SENELEC, the power utility, and unexpectedly low personal income tax compliance.[25] In order to implement the PSE as planned, Senegal must ensure consistent revenue mobilization. A few measures taken by the government include a special 45 percent tax on cigarettes, increasing the minimum flat tax, a review of the personal income tax, and a one percent levy of all turnover of telecommunications companies.[26]

These measures coincide with drastic spending cuts within the federal state, including the closing of 16 government agencies and the merging of eight agencies into three.[27] At the same time, Senegal has underinvested in certain areas of government. As of 2009, Senegal had about one tax agency staff member for every 14,000 citizens. This is extremely low, particularly in comparison to other West African countries.

In spite of Senegal's overall positive trajectory, businesses still experience severe challenges that hinder potential growth. Senegal ranks poorly on the World Bank's Doing Business Index, at 178 out of 189 economies. Possibly as a result, many reforms today focus on improving the business environment, particularly for small- and medium-sized enterprises (SMEs). Significant portions of tax reforms in the 2013 budget relate to the tax hurdles and overall difficult environment facing SMEs. A 2012 African Development Bank report cites "lengthy tax formalities" as a key factor hindering SME development in Senegal. The country is ranked still lower in the Doing Business Paying Taxes index, at 182. Businesses in Senegal

23. Republic of Senegal, "Plan Senegal Emergent, PSE 2014–2018," February 2014, http://www.gcsenegal.gouv.sn/docs/Resume_PSE.pdf.
24. Republic of Senegal, "Plan Senegal Emergent: Plan d'Actions Prioritaires," February 2014, http://www.gcsenegal.gouv.sn/docs/PAP%202014-2018%20%20du%20PSE%20version%20definitive%20commentaires%20et%20ANNEXES.pdf.
25. IMF, "Senegal Seventh Review Under the Policy Support Instrument and Request for Modification of Assessment Criteria—Staff Report; and Press Release," 9.
26. Ibid., 26.
27. Ibid., 28.

can expect to spend 644 hours preparing, filing, and paying taxes, as compared to 314 hours average in sub-Saharan Africa and 175 hours in OECD countries.[28]

Senegal also continues to improve the corporate tax environment through cooperation with the Investment Climate Facility for Africa (ICF), a group that works with governments to make business friendly reforms to attract investment. ICF is working with the government of Senegal to streamline the country's tax administration system with the aim of saving resources and time of the private sector. Specific reforms include digitalizing tax records and reducing the processing time of corporate and VAT refunds from over 175 days to 30 days.[29]

Senegal is one of the six founding members of the Collaborative Africa Budget Reform Initiative (CABRI), an organization founded in 2009 that promotes efficient and effective management of public finances.[30] CABRI is a legally distinct entity that works closely with African governments and played a key role in aid effectiveness conversations at the Busan High Level Forum on Aid Effectiveness.[31] CABRI and USAID are currently working together to lead a dialogue on the use of local or country systems to improve domestic ownership and accountability.[32]

While Senegal still struggles to widen its tax base and increase domestic revenue flows, the Senegalese government is taking promising steps to continue on a path of stable financial management. With responsible deficit management throughout the PSE process, Senegal should continue to serve as a model for future reforms in West Africa.

Chile

The past 15 years have demonstrated a significant rise in efforts by tax administrations around the world to implement electronic filing due to the system's reduced costs and processing times. E-filing also provides a number of benefits for users, allowing taxpayers to conduct their tax payment activities and access tax-related information in a more convenient and timely manner. Ideally, a transition to an online-based tax administration system would provide a degree of flexibility, accuracy, and cost efficiency for both the government and taxpayers that would not otherwise be available through traditional channels.

---

28. World Bank, *Doing Business 2014: Economy Profile: Senegal* (Washington, DC: World Bank, 2014), 64–70, http://www.doingbusiness.org/data/exploreeconomies/senegal/~/media/giawb/doing%20business/documents/profiles/country/SEN.pdf?ver=2.
29. Investment Climate Facility for Africa (ICF), "Large companies in Senegal now pay their taxes online," March 10, 2014, http://www.icfafrica.org/news/large-companies-in-senegal-now-pay-their-taxes-online.
30. Collaborative Africa Budget Reform Initiatives (CABRI), "Senegal," 2013, http://cabri-sbo.org/where-we-work/western-africa/senegal.
31. Deutsche Gesellschaft für Internationale Zusammenarbeit (GIZ), "Transparent and Responsible Public Finances: Good Financial Governance in Africa," June 2014, http://www.giz.de/en/downloads/giz2014-en-transparent-responsible-public-finances-gfg-africa.pdf.
32. Effective Institutions Platform, "Country Dialogues for Using and Strengthening Local Systems: Proposal from Pillar III," n.d., http://www.effectiveinstitutions.org/documentupload/Pillar_III_Proposal.pdf.

A study by McKinsey & Co. confirms the benefits of e-filing, correlating high e-filing rates with increased full-time equivalent, or workload, efficiency.[33] However, it notes that a tax administration accrues the full benefit of the online system only when it reaches close to a 100 percent e-filing rate.[34] This is due to the fact that the costs associated with processing the remaining paper returns are far more expensive than all other aspects of the e-filing system. As e-filing levels approach closer to 100 percent, the labor-intensive resources and the facilities dedicated to processing paper returns become increasingly unnecessary. The study shows that countries with e-filing rates above 98 percent are substantially more efficient than countries even with rates as high as 90 percent.[35]

Chile is one of the few countries that has successfully come close to achieving this goal, at a 97 percent e-filing rate, and can be considered a leader among Latin American and Caribbean (LAC) countries in terms of tax administration efficiency. In 2003, Chile's tax administration, Chile Servicio de Impuestos Internos (SII), won the United Nations Good Practices and Innovations in Public Governance Award for its web-based tax management system. The system offers a platform that enables taxpayers to complete the entire tax payment process online and also provides users with information regarding tax regulations, filing procedures, and international investments.[36] The website further includes a portal for businesses of all sizes to obtain electronic tax documents at no cost and acts as a portal for Tax Education, teaching children and youths about taxes and their social benefits.

SII introduced its web-based tax management system in 1999. However, not long after its introduction, the administration was faced with a number of challenges that threatened its initial ability to boost e-filing rates. Internet connectivity was sparse throughout the country, and when attainable, often came at a high cost for usage. Because of low education levels, the general population relied heavily on accountants and tax preparers, who themselves were reluctant to accept e-filing because of their unfamiliarity with the service. There was also a widespread perception that the online system might pose a threat to their profession. Additionally, even as the tax administration began promoting the e-filing platform, internal IT systems had not yet developed the capacity to prepare for the massive congestion that resulted in the days immediately prior to the deadline.

In order to overcome these barriers, Chile implemented initiatives to increase compliance and access to the new systems. A number of partnerships with regional shopping centers and national telecom service providers allowed for the creation of a national public-private network. The subsequent establishment of a network of more than 880 centers, located at shopping malls, offices of the revenue body, and mobile access points, provided

33. Thomas Dohrmann and Gary Pinshaw, *The Road to Improved Compliance: A McKinsey Benchmarking Study of Tax Administrations—2008–2009* (Washington, DC: McKinsey & Co., September 2009).

34. Ibid., 13.

35. Ibid.

36. Arturo Jacobs et al., *Detailed Guidelines for Improved Tax Administration in Latin America and the Caribbean* (Washington, DC: USAID, August 2013), 120, http://www.usaid.gov/sites/default/files/LAC_TaxBook_Entire%20Book%20-%20ENGLISH.pdf.

up to 3,000 internet connectivity points for taxpayers without access to the Web at home.[37] By 2007, more than half of the new e-filings had been submitted via these networks. Additionally, the government formed agreements with Internet cafés that allowed taxpayers to make online submissions at no cost. They also designated specific weeks for mobile units with computers and tax agents to travel to different parts of the country and help people file their taxes online. Finally, they launched aggressive marketing and awareness campaigns to increase the use of these access points.[38]

Additionally, the Chilean government offered incentives for taxpayers to file their returns online. Online filers would be offered early refunds on their returns. Further, by improving accessibility to the web, submitting tax-related inquiries online was up to eight times cheaper than calling a revenue branch for telephone assistance. Finally, taxpayers who chose not to adopt the online system were obligated to submit their tax forms in person at tax-administration branches or kiosks.[39] However, this process was also streamlined as a result of e-filing. Because an increasing number of taxpayers chose to file their returns online and because the online process greatly improved the accuracy of tax collection, tax officers stationed in office branches had more time to commit to those who did choose to turn in their tax forms in person. Consequently, the SII was able to implement the "Maximum Waiting Time" project that guarantees taxpayers who come into tax-administration branches a maximum waiting period of 30 minutes. If this time limit is exceeded, an official from the service will take the relevant documents, process the request, and mail them back to the taxpayer's home for free.[40]

The online system proved to be successful, boosting total tax revenues from US$13,591.3 million in 1999 to US$55,961.5 million in 2012 (see Figure 1).[41] The e-filing rate has also grown from 5 percent in 1999 to 97 percent in 2007, taking over as the primary form of tax filing used. A significant portion of this success can be attributed to the system's heavy investment in personnel who carry out core functions. Personnel accounts for over 80 percent of the Chilean tax administration's total costs,[42] as the government dedicates significant resources towards educational courses for its employees. Since the mid-1990s, 2,500 people have annually spent over 100,000 hours in training.[43]

---

37. Forum on Tax Administration, *Strategies for Improving the Take-up Rates of Electronic Services* (Paris: OECD, March 2006), http://www.oecd.org/tax/administration/36280699.pdf.

38. Dohrmann and Pinshaw, *The Road to Improved Compliance*, 16.

39. Ibid.

40. Pablo Serra, "Measuring the Performance of Chile's Tax Administration," *National Tax Journal* LVI, no. 2 (June 2003): 373–383, http://www.ntanet.org/NTJ/56/2/ntj-v56n02p373-83-measuring-performance-chile-tax.pdf; Paul Constance, "Simplify, Simplify, Simplify and then buy the computers," Inter-American Development Bank, March 1, 2002, http://www.iadb.org/en/news/webstories/2002-03-01/simplify-simplify-simplify-and-then-buy-the-computers,8941.html.

41. OECD StatExtracts, "Revenue Statistics—Comparative tables," accessed September 25, 2014, http://stats.oecd.org/Index.aspx?DataSetCode=REV.

42. Inter-American Development Bank, Regional Technical Assistance Center for Central America, Panama and Dominican Republic, and Inter-American Center of Tax Administrations, *State of the Tax Administration in Latin America: 2006–2010* (Washington, DC: Inter-American Development Bank, 2013), 19, http://publications.iadb.org/bitstream/handle/11319/3506/State%20of%20the%20TA%20in%20LATAM%202006-2010.pdf?sequence=7.

43. Predrag Bejakovic, "Improving the Tax Administration in Transition Countries," January 2001, http://www.umar.gov.si/fileadmin/user_upload/konference/06/10_bejakovic.pdf, 13.

Figure 1. Total Tax Revenues in Chile, 1990–2011

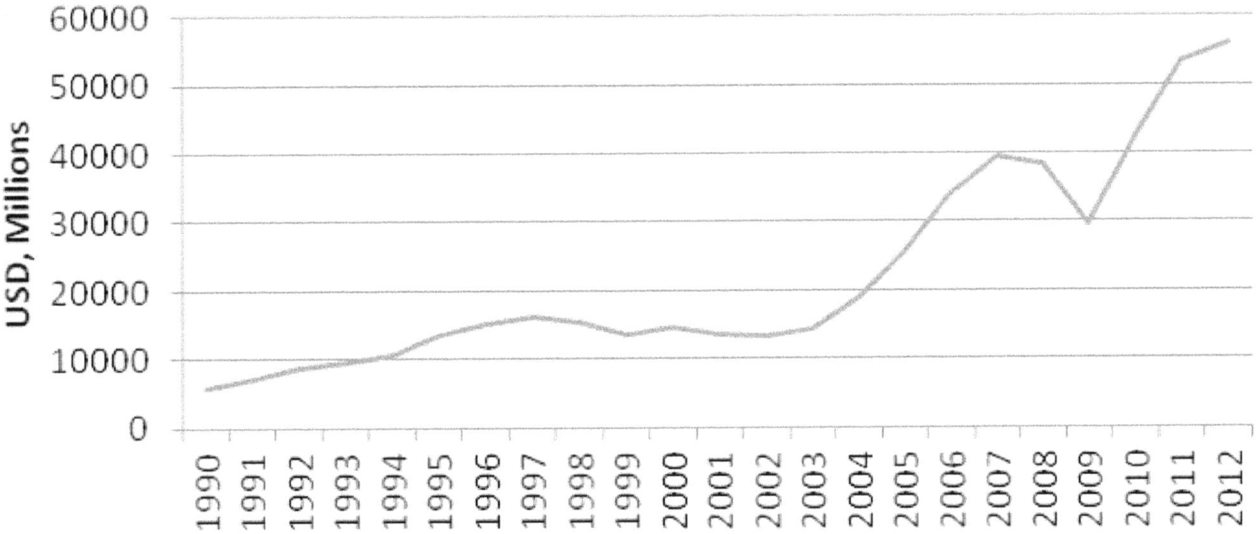

Perhaps even more significant, however, is Chile's initiative to reward its tax collectors based on their collection efforts. Using performance from the previous year as a benchmark, employees can achieve bonuses of between 13.5 percent and 27 percent of their salary, depending on the position of the staff member concerned. Additionally, each year the best-appraised third of the staff receive a bonus equivalent to 4 percent of the salary, and the next third obtains 2 percent.[44] Despite this high incentive scheme, there have been few reported incidents of corruption. This can perhaps be attributed to the selective nature of tax managers in the SII. When Javier Etcheberry assumed presidency of the tax administration in 1990, he handpicked the SII's top 150 managers strictly on the basis of their qualifications. Finally, he implemented a much more rigorous performance review program for all staff members.[45]

The incentive scheme, paired with the robust staff, is thought to be accountable for the administration's reputable efficiency, particularly in the Latin America and Caribbean region. Chile's tax administration has 146 employees per percentage point of GDP collected and processes an average of 899 reports per employee. By contrast, Argentina's tax administration has 1,000 employees per percentage point of GDP and processes only 277 tax reports per employee.[46]

Despite these efficiencies, however, the tax evasion rates in Chile are still remarkably high. Between 2001 and 2006, Chile suffered from a 47.4 percent total income tax evasion rate.[47]

---

44. Serra, "Measuring the Performance of Chile's Tax Administration," 374.
45. Constance, "Simplify, Simplify, Simplify and then buy the computers."
46. Nancy Birdsall, Augusto de la Torre, and Rachel Menezes, *Fair Growth: Economic Policies for Latin America's Poor and Middle-Income Majority* (Washington, DC: Center for Global Development, 2008), 10, http://www.cgdev.org/sites/default/files/15192_file_fairGrowth_entire_0.pdf.
47. Juan Carlos Gómez Sabaini and Juan Pablo Jiménez, *Tax Structure and Tax Evasion in Latin America* (Santiago: United Nations, February 2012), 34, http://www.cepal.org/publicaciones/xml/5/45935/SERIE_MD_118.pdf.

Evasion of the corporate income tax was also extensive, at 48.4 percent, while the individual income tax evasion rate was slightly lower at 46 percent. Because there have been very few empirical investigations surrounding the reasons for tax evasion in the region,[48] it is difficult to determine the exact causes for these figures. However, it can be presumed that a significant portion of these figures simply reflect tax avoidance on the side of corporations and individuals, and a low probability of detection and low costs for noncompliance on the side of the Chilean government. This is supported by the fact that the VAT evasion rate in Chile is significantly lower (and is, in fact, the lowest VAT evasion rate in all of Latin America) at only 11 percent[49] because the tax administration has taken on significant measures to study and target VAT evasions. Chile is one of the few countries in Latin America where the tax administration measures evasion of the VAT on an annual basis and then sets goals to reduce noncompliance in this area.[50] Between the years of 1990 and 1999 alone, the Chilean government was able to reduce the VAT evasion rate from 28 percent to 20 percent after implementing differentiated strategies to tackle the high number.[51] Provided the appropriate strategies and implementation, perhaps a similar effect can be achieved in reducing income tax evasion as well. Increasing audit rates would increase the likelihood of detecting noncompliance, and thus incentivize individuals and corporations against tax evasion. Alternatively, the tax administration could be shrewder in their selection of taxpayers for audit. By using statistical data analysis, the administration could focus audit efforts on individuals that are most likely to evade. Increasing the costs for noncompliance could similarly dissuade individuals and corporations from evading tax responsibilities.

Nevertheless, the story of Chile's transition from a paper-based tax administration to a streamlined web-based platform should serve as a model for other governments hoping to establish an e-filing system. The latest study conducted in 2000 revealed that despite the fact that only 860,000 people in Chile have access to the Internet, more than 85 percent of that number, around 734,000 of the country's 2 million corporate and individual taxpayers, are using the online platform to complete their tax business.[52] This makes the SII website one of the most visited websites in the country. With a 272 percent growth in tax revenue between the year of the implementation of the e-filing system (1999) and 2011, there is no denying that the increased convenience, accuracy, and cost efficiency of the program has significant benefits. The challenge now is to use the technology to continue promoting tax compliance, while ensuring that the tax administration becomes even more efficient and transparent.

48. Birdsall et al., *Fair Growth*, 10.

49. Gomez Sabaini and Jiménez, *Tax Structure and Tax Evasion in Latin America*, 34.

50. Ibid., 32.

51. Barrie Russell, *Revenue Administration: Developing a Taxpayer Compliance Program* (Washington, DC: IMF, November 2010), 13, https://www.imf.org/external/pubs/ft/tnm/2010/tnm1017.pdf.

52. Liselott Kana, "Taxing time for e-government," *OECD Observer*, October 13, 2914, http://www.oecdobserver.org/news/archivestory.php/aid/424/Taxing_time_for_e-government.html.

Conclusion and Recommendations

It has become commonplace to accept that international development has changed tremendously over the past two decades; no more so than in the field of financing for development. Although this is often stated to highlight the growing role that the private sector—both international and local—is playing in development, stakeholders frequently overlook the growing amount of domestic resources that are available for countries to pay for their own development. But beyond simply paying for development, domestic resources, whether through avenues such as taxation or the growing number of countries that can tap sovereign capital markets, offer an important path for countries to truly take ownership of their own development and fulfill the social compact that is at the heart of good governance.

To be sure, DRM is a growing part of the international dialogue on development cooperation. It has been part of the discussion at Paris, Accra, and Busan, and is now a central pillar of the Global Partnership for Effective Development Cooperation. This, above all else, has been the most important piece of the evolving donor focus on DRM. For better or for worse, the Global Partnership is the international imprimatur for how donors approach specific development issues. By raising DRM to the level of a pillar of this partnership, bilateral and multilateral donors have the rhetorical cover to devote significant time and resources toward DRM. Moreover, by increasing a country's ability to generate greater revenues to pay for its own development, this also fosters country ownership—a central focus of the Global Partnership conversation. After all, taxes and expenditures directed toward its own priorities is the ultimate expression of a country's ownership of its development trajectory.

It is important, though, to not simply treat DRM as a technocratic problem that can be solved through additional technical assistance missions. Ultimately, reforming tax systems, increasing taxpayer participation, and generating greater revenue for the state is about tackling persistent governance challenges in developing countries. Any attempt to reform these systems cannot be accomplished without consistent political support from the government and political leadership. Of particular concern for developing countries is the narrowness of the groups involved in debate over taxation and public expenditure. Those who do engage are frequently the political and economic elite of a country and have a strong incentive to resist change. This serves to weaken governance and the rule of law in these countries; by seeking to engage with a broader swath of the citizenry, a government will improve its accountability and transparency.

There is no shortage of information on how to approach to reforming tax systems, increasing DRM, or improving public financial management. The IMF and OECD have emerged over the last decade as a leading force for the reforms needed to enhance DRM, and the international community should continue to leverage their influence and convening power to secure greater donor and country commitments to DRM. The United States, as the world's leading donor, should play a larger role in advocating for and advancing a new development focus on domestic resources. In considering how to approach this, the U.S. government should do the following.

Recommendation 1: Place DRM and public financial management at the center of a renewed effort around good governance.

Good governance remains one of the most important challenges facing developing countries; at the center of this is increased accountability toward citizens. Increasing the domestic resources available allows countries to more ably govern and provide necessary public goods and services. The U.S. government should incorporate DRM in governance efforts by:

- Securing commitments and establishing criteria for countries to meet as conditions for continued or enhanced development assistance; and
- Reaching consensus on metrics by which to establish DRM baselines and measure progress over time.

Recommendation 2: Increase commitments to DRM on a bilateral level and to multidonor trust funds.

At one percent of global foreign assistance, support for DRM reforms reflects the low priority many donors have attached to it. At the April High-Level Meeting in Mexico City, donors endorsed a call to double the total amount of ODA committed to DRM; this is a commitment that should be carried out in the coming year.

For the United States, this would mean increasing its current DRM spending of approximately $35 million per year to $70 million per year. This is a good goal, but the U.S. government should go further and increase support to $200 million per year. Secretary Kerry's announcement at the Frontiers in Development conference is a good first step and one that should be built upon in the coming year. In order to do so, the United States should do the following:

- To find additional money to support this renewed effort, the U.S. government should identify a percentage of existing earmarks within the existing foreign aid budget similar to the recent announcement by Secretary Kerry. This would mean dedicating a portion of not just of Congressional earmarks, but also funding for presidential initiatives (e.g., PEPFAR, Feed the Future, etc.) to DRM.

- Consider adding a DRM and public financial management project to all future MCC compacts, in particular, second generation compacts; as well as to future Partnership for Growth (PFG) or PFG-like bilateral compacts, such as the one already in place in the Philippines.
- Increase support for initiatives such as the Collaborative African Budget Reform Initiative (CABRI).

Recommendation 3: Donors should tie the use of local systems to a corresponding commitment to improve public financial management and tax systems in order to mobilize additional domestic resources.

Since the 2005 Paris Declaration, donors have committed themselves to the increased use of local systems with a particular emphasis on the use of "country systems," which is commonly understood to mean a recipient government's systems; that is, general or sector budget support. There are significant risks involved in the increased use of local government financial management systems, which must be addressed and considered if donors are to make greater use of them. Going forward, donors should incorporate specific reform programs into the greater use of general or sector budget support. This should include a commitment by the host country to tackle any political or economic reforms that are necessary, technical assistance for the reform of systems, and support training of government personnel. The future use of local systems should be conditioned on specific benchmarks agreed to by the donor and host country.

Appendix: Revenue Mobilization by Country

Peru[1]

Peru	*Total Revenue (USD, millions)*	*Revenue, Tax (USD, millions)*	*Revenue, Social Contributions (USD, millions)*	*Revenue, Grants (USD, millions)*	*Revenue, Other (USD, millions)*
2001	8823	6258	NA	NA	2565
2002	9179	6425	NA	NA	2754
2003	10064	7404	NA	NA	2661
2004	11498	8673	NA	NA	2825
2005	13347	10084	NA	NA	3263
2006	17423	13221	NA	NA	4203
2007	21150	16041	NA	NA	5109
2008	25369	18936	NA	NA	6433
2009	22423	17090	2303	0	3030
2010	29999	22573	2673	0	4752
2011	35989	27120	3241	171	5458
2012	41802	31592	3853	193	6164
2013	43089	32367	4046	0	6676

1. Metrics are taken from IMF, "Peru and the IMF: Article IV Staff Reports," 2001–2013, http://www.imf.org/external/country/per/index.htm?type=9998#56. Final numbers were arrived at by multiplying metric as percent of GDP by GDP, as given in World Bank, "World Development Indicators: Peru," http://databank.worldbank.org/data/views/variableSelection/selectvariables.aspx?source=world-development-indicators.

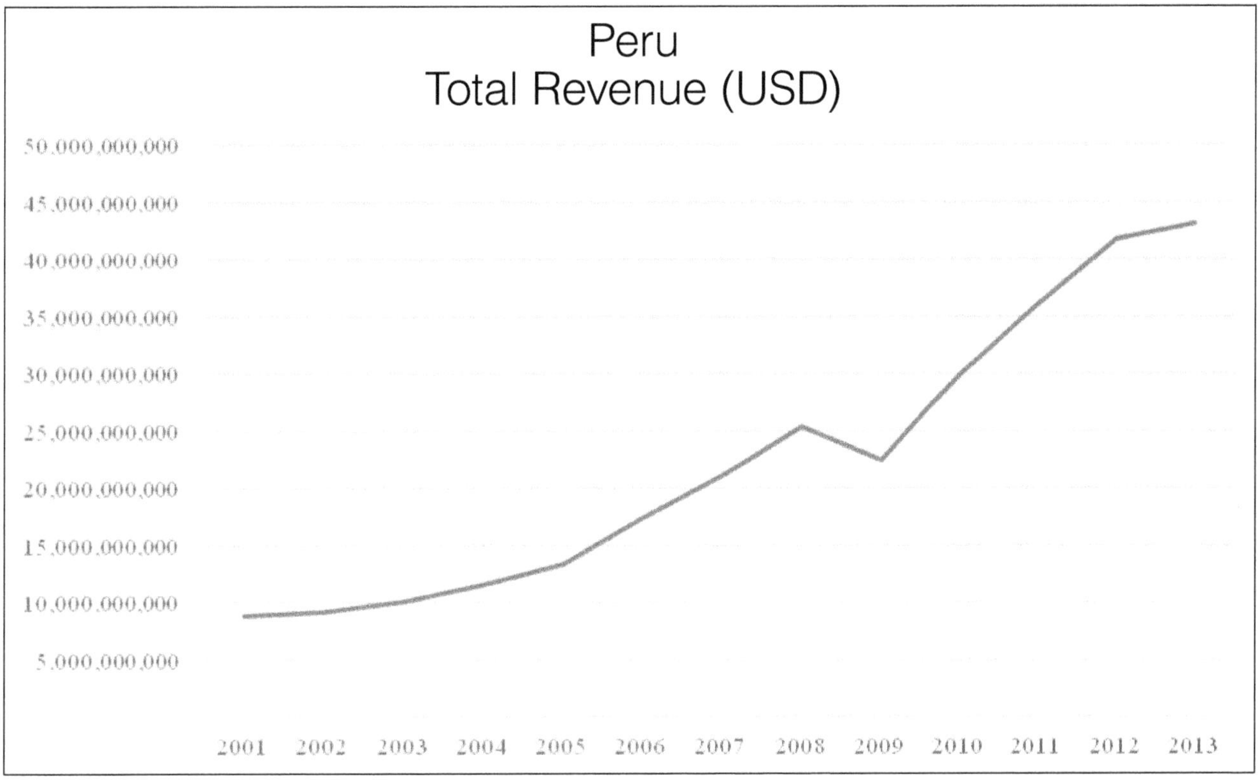
Peru
Total Revenue (USD)
50,000,000,000
45,000,000,000
40,000,000,000
35,000,000,000
30,000,000,000
25,000,000,000
20,000,000,000
15,000,000,000
10,000,000,000
5,000,000,000
2001 2002 2003 2004 2005 2006 2007 2008 2009 2010 2011 2012 2013

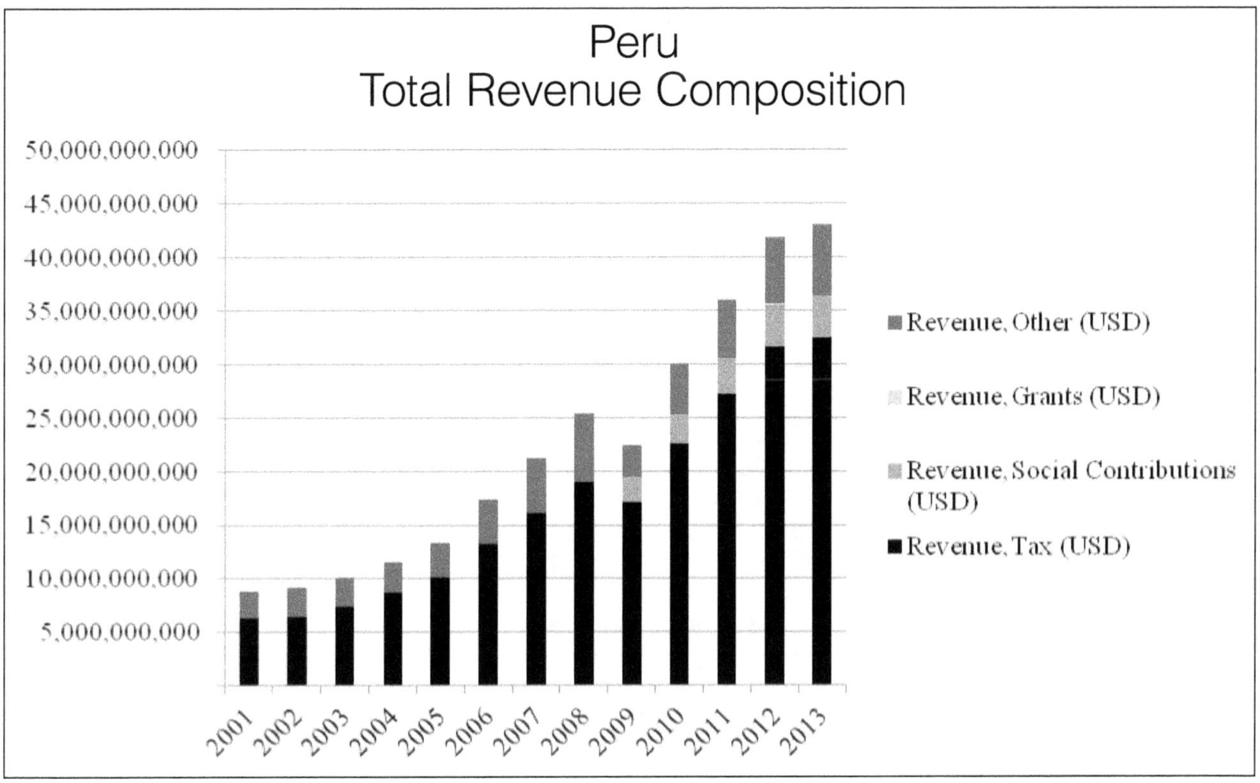
Peru
Total Revenue Composition
50,000,000,000
45,000,000,000
40,000,000,000
35,000,000,000
30,000,000,000
25,000,000,000
20,000,000,000
15,000,000,000
10,000,000,000
5,000,000,000
2001 2002 2003 2004 2005 2006 2007 2008 2009 2010 2011 2012 2013
Revenue, Other (USD)
Revenue, Grants (USD)
Revenue, Social Contributions (USD)
Revenue, Tax (USD)

El Salvador[2]

El Salvador	*Total Revenue (USD, millions)*	*Revenue, Tax (USD, millions)*	*Revenue, Non-Tax (USD, millions)*	*Revenue, Grants (USD, millions)*	*Revenue, Other (USD, millions)*
2001	2141	1450	566	55	69
2002	2289	1602	572	43	72
2003	2483	1730	572	75	105
2004	2528	1833	553	47	95
2005	2820	2137	547	51	85
2006	3191	2467	557	37	130
2007	3438	2694	583	60	101
2008	3729	2893	621	43	171
2009	3388	2603	579	103	103
2010	3812	2891	643	171	107
2011	4234	3193	648	208	185
2012	4501	3429	738	167	167
2013	4731	3712	776	73	170

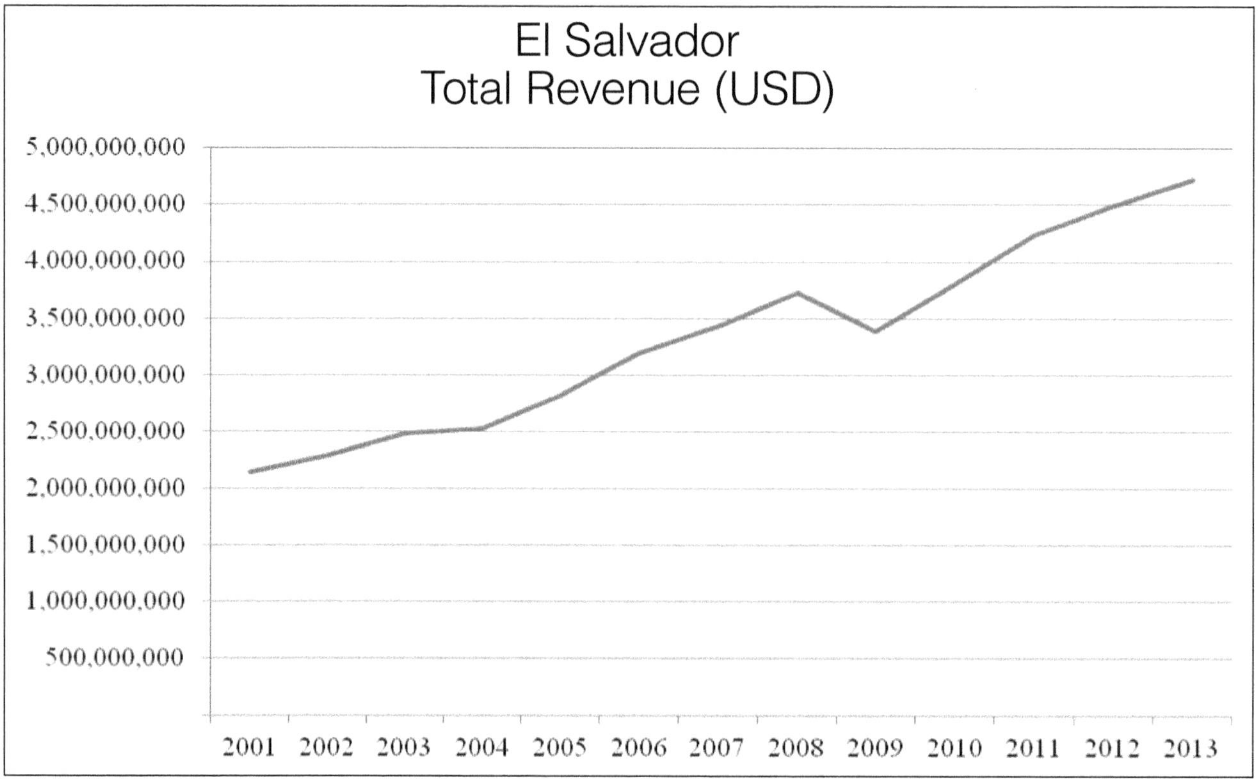

2. Metrics taken from IMF, "El Salvador: 2013 Article IV Consultation," May 2013, http://www.imf.org/external/pubs/ft/scr/2013/cr13132.pdf. Final numbers were arrived at by multiplying metric as percent of GDP by GDP, as given in World Bank, "World Development Indicators: El Salvador," http://databank.worldbank.org/data/views/variableSelection/selectvariables.aspx?source=world-development-indicators.

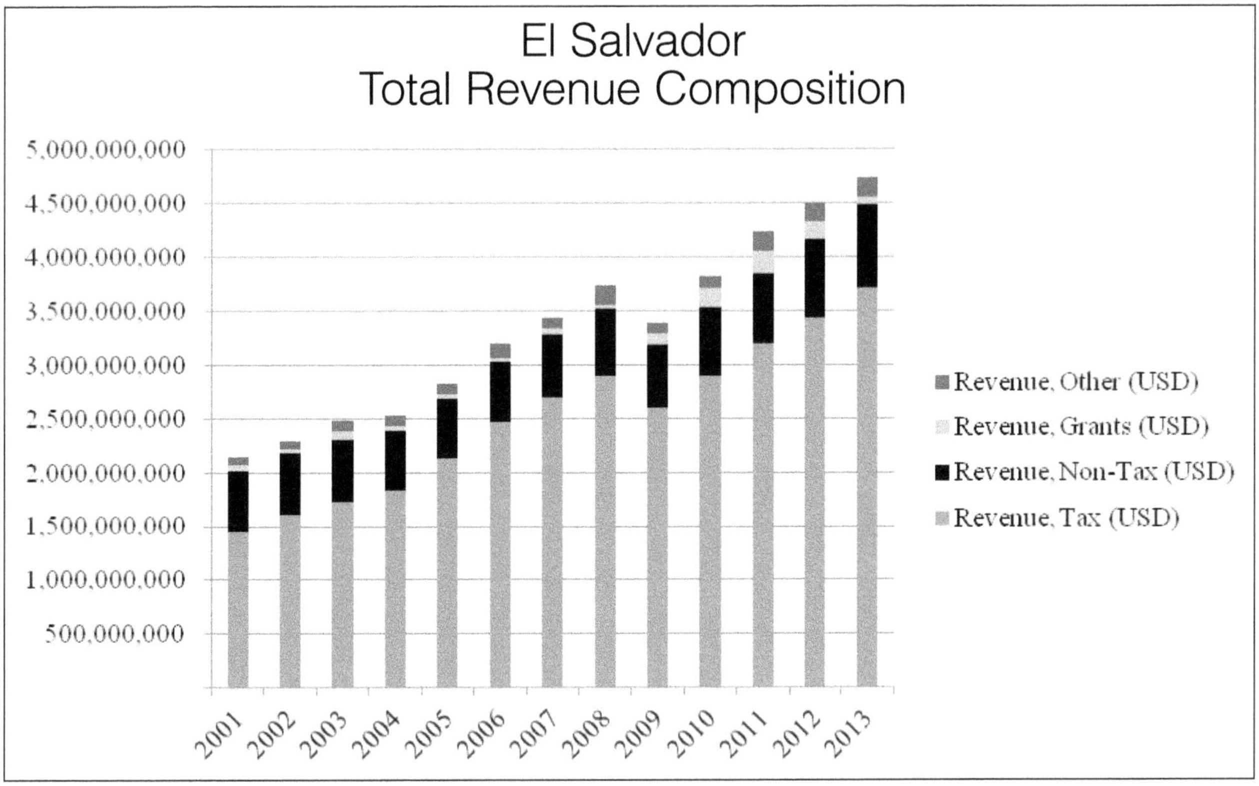

Costa Rica[3]

Costa Rica	*Total Revenue (USD, millions)*	*Revenue, Tax Overall (USD, millions)*	*Revenue, Direct Taxes (USD, millions)*	*Revenue, Sales Taxes (USD, millions)*	*Revenue, Non-Tax (USD, millions)*	*Revenue, Other (USD, millions)*
2001	3691	2182	607	804	33	1476
2002	3756	2223	640	825	17	1516
2003	3976	2382	701	823	53	1542
2004	4110	2492	744	911	56	1562
2005	4532	2715	819	1018	60	1757
2006	4776	3154	901	1216	45	1577
2007	6159	4001	1211	1553	342	1816
2008	7040	4683	1521	1790	298	2058
2009	6611	4025	NA	NA	382	2204
2010	8058	4864	NA	NA	472	2722
2011	9278	5732	NA	NA	536	3010
2012	11026	7124	NA	NA	590	3312

3. Metrics taken from IMF, "Costa Rica: 2012 Article IV Consultation," March 2013, http://www.imf.org/external/pubs/ft/scr/2013/cr1379.pdf. Final numbers were arrived at by multiplying metric as percent of GDP by GDP, as given in World Bank, "World Development Indicators: Costa Rica," http://databank.worldbank.org/data/views/variableSelection/selectvariables.aspx?source=world-development-indicators.

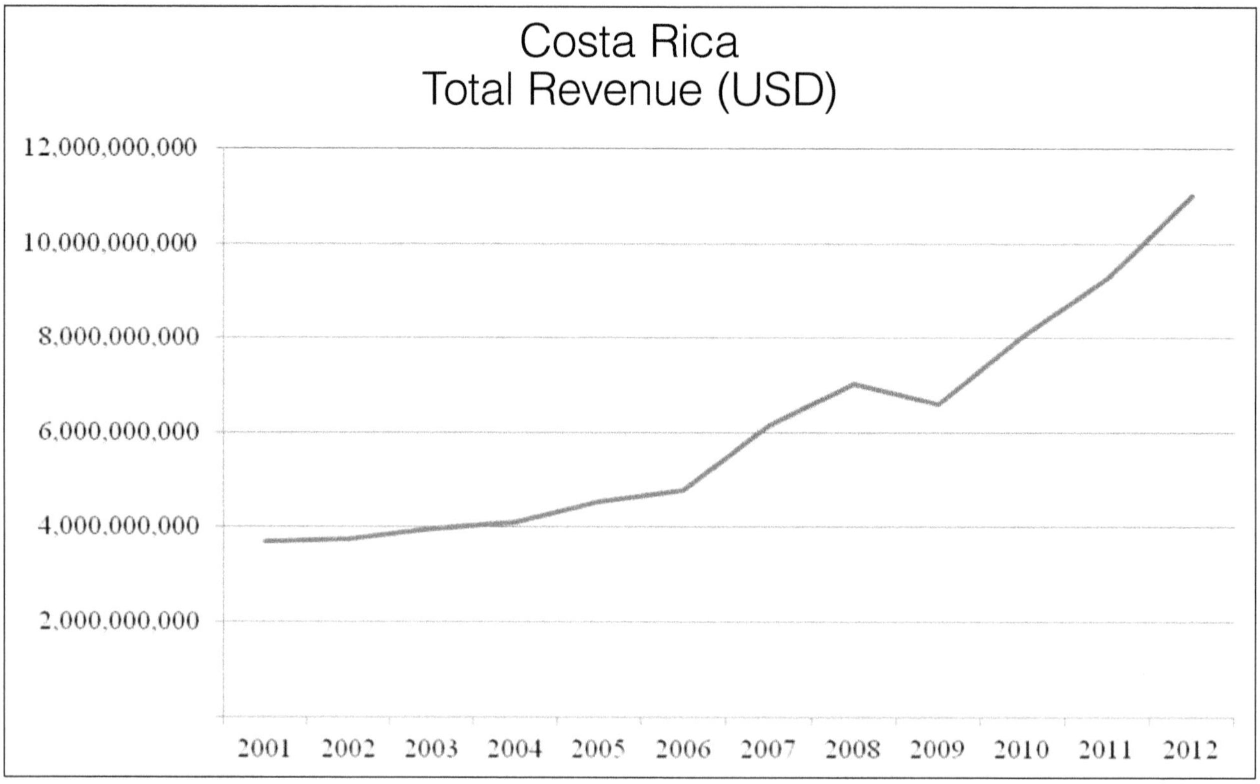

Costa Rica
Total Revenue (USD)
12,000,000,000
10,000,000,000
8,000,000,000
6,000,000,000
4,000,000,000
2,000,000,000
2001
2002
2003
2004
2005
2006
2007
2008
2009
2010
2011
2012

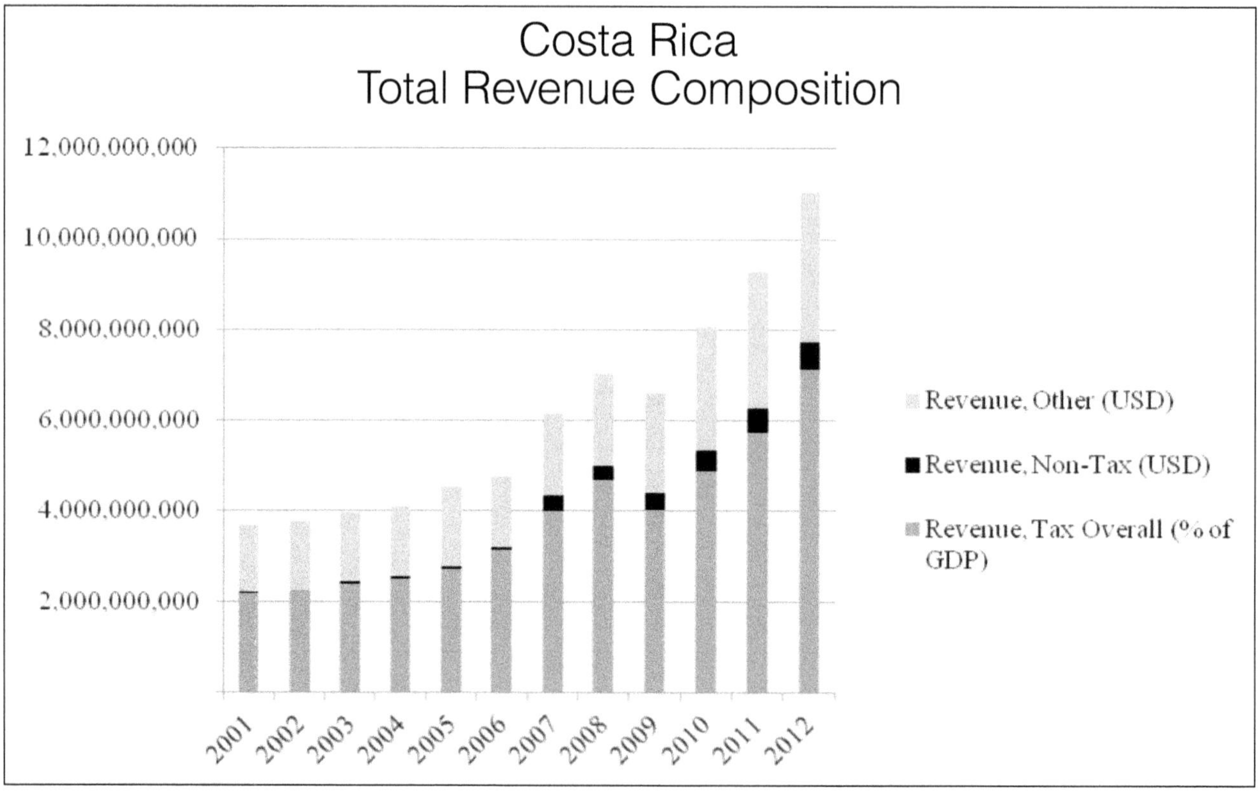

Costa Rica
Total Revenue Composition
12,000,000,000
10,000,000,000
8,000,000,000
6,000,000,000
4,000,000,000
2,000,000,000
2001
2002
2003
2004
2005
2006
2007
2008
2009
2010
2011
2012
Revenue, Other (USD)
Revenue, Non-Tax (USD)
Revenue, Tax Overall (% of GDP)

Chile[4]

Chile	*Total Revenue (USD, millions)*	*Revenue, Taxes (USD, millions)*	*Revenue, Social Contributions (USD, millions)*	*Revenue, Grants (USD, millions)*	*Revenue, Other (USD, millions)*
2001	15769	12008	1013	217	2532
2002	14978	11854	1065	142	1917
2003	16191	12377	1090	156	2569
2004	22340	15799	1409	101	5032
2005	29608	21024	1742	249	6593
2006	39905	26294	2011	309	11291
2007	46539	32525	2249	346	11418
2008	45864	33274	2518	360	9712
2009	32741	23953	2413	172	6204
2010	46763	34583	2828	218	9135
2011	57014	43702	3265	251	9795
2012	59110	46862	3728	266	8254
2013	57935	46292	3881	277	7484

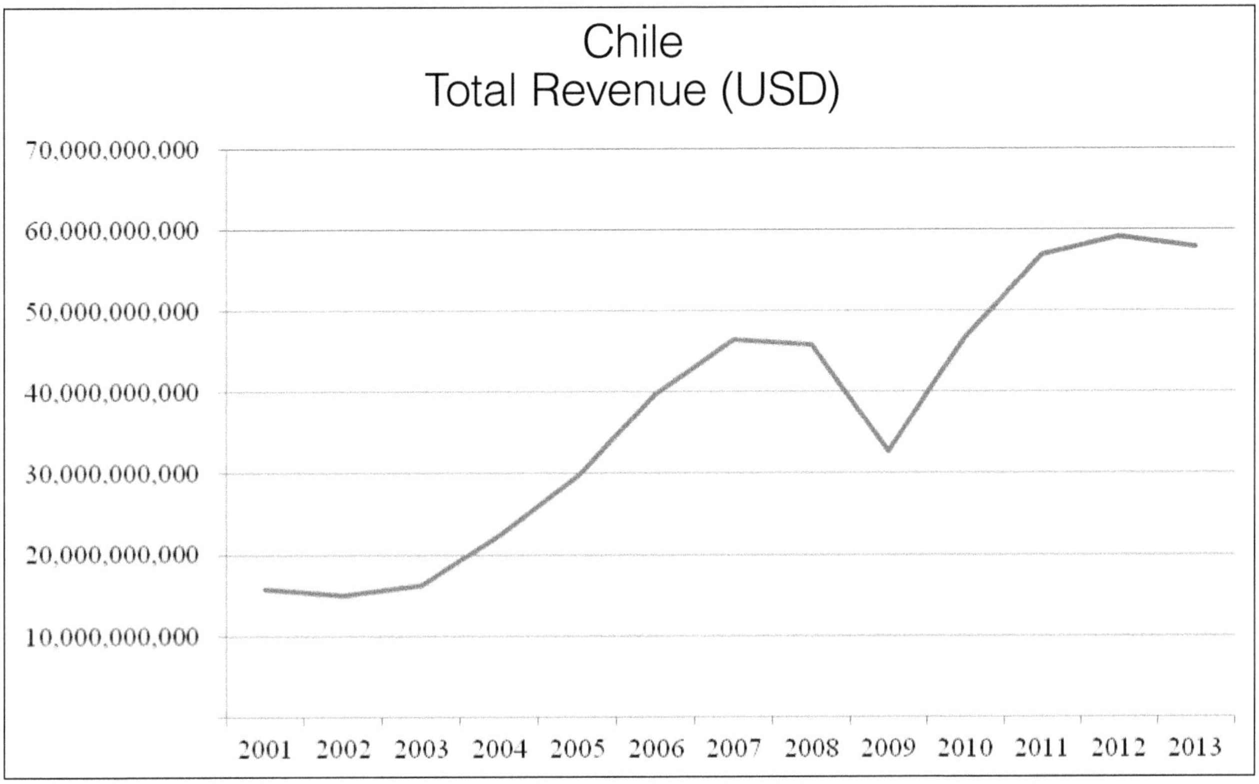

4. Metrics taken from IMF, "Chile: 2013 Article IV Consultation," July 2013, http://www.imf.org/external/pubs/ft/scr/2013/cr13198.pdf. Final numbers were arrived at by multiplying metric as percent of GDP by GDP, as given in World Bank, "World Development Indicators: Chile," http://databank.worldbank.org/data/views/variableSelection/selectvariables.aspx?source=world-development-indicators.

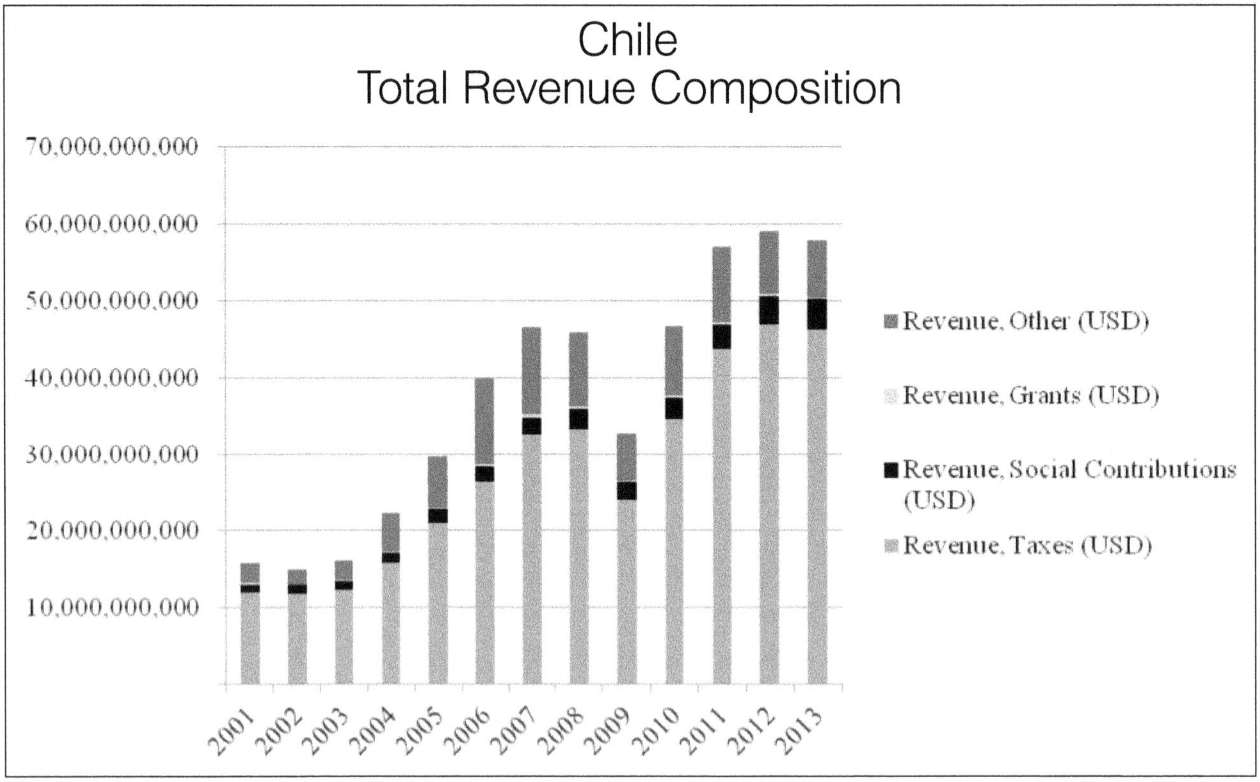

Indonesia[5]

Indonesia	*Total Revenue (USD, millions)*	*Revenue, Tax (USD, millions)*	*Revenue, Grants (USD, millions)*	*Revenue, Other (USD, millions)*
2001	28720	18612	NA	10108
2002	31501	23088	NA	8413
2003	38503	29112	NA	9391
2004	45460	31591	Na	13869
2005	51170	35734	NA	15437
2006	68539	44842	365	23697
2007	77367	53595	NA	23772
2008	97457	66332	NA	31125
2009	81477	61512	NA	19964
2010	112052	82266	NA	29786
2011	136195	99820	NA	36375
2012	142029	104330	877	37699
2013	138067	105938	NA	32129

5. Metrics taken from IMF, "Indonesia: Staff Report for the 2013 Article IV Consultation," December 2013, http://www.imf.org/external/pubs/ft/scr/2013/cr13362.pdf. Final numbers were arrived at by multiplying metric as percent of GDP by GDP, as given in World Bank, "World Development Indicators: Indonesia," http://databank.worldbank.org/data/views/variableSelection/selectvariables.aspx?source=world-development-indicators.

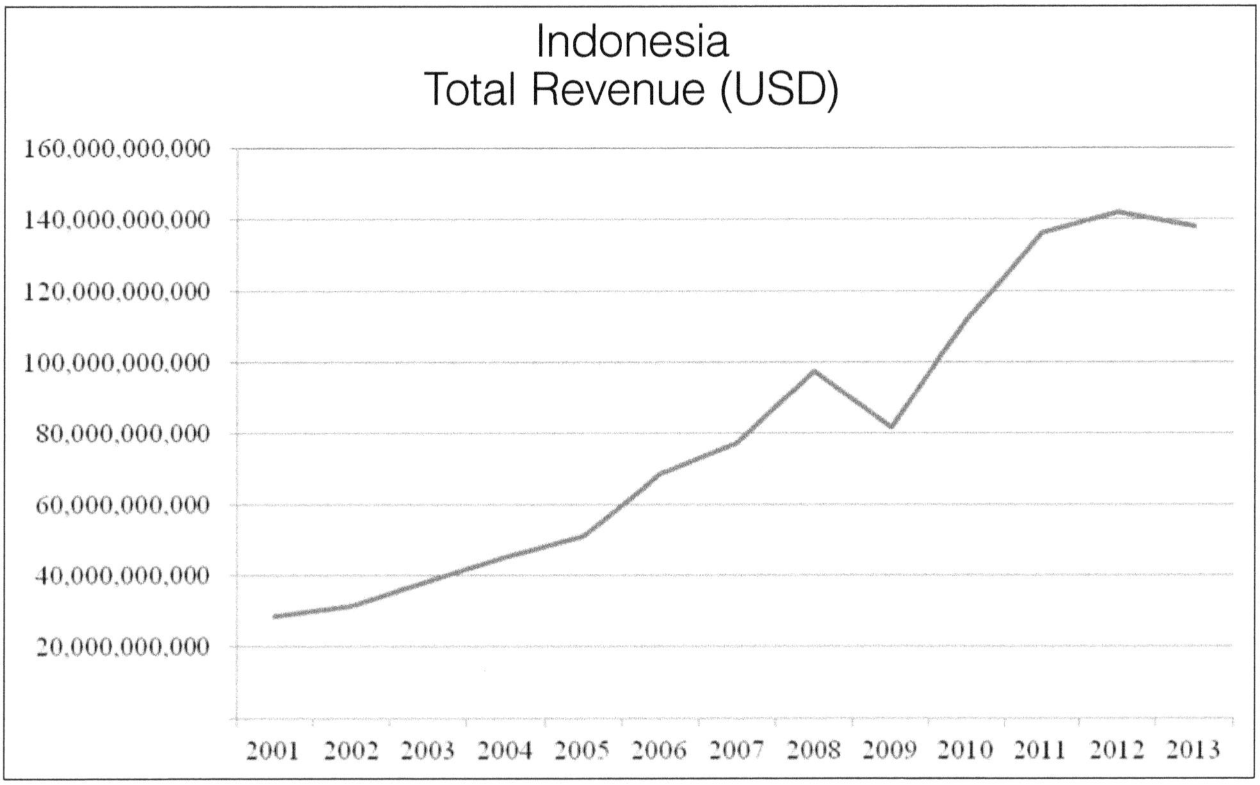
Indonesia
Total Revenue (USD)
160,000,000,000
140,000,000,000
120,000,000,000
100,000,000,000
80,000,000,000
60,000,000,000
40,000,000,000
20,000,000,000
2001 2002 2003 2004 2005 2006 2007 2008 2009 2010 2011 2012 2013

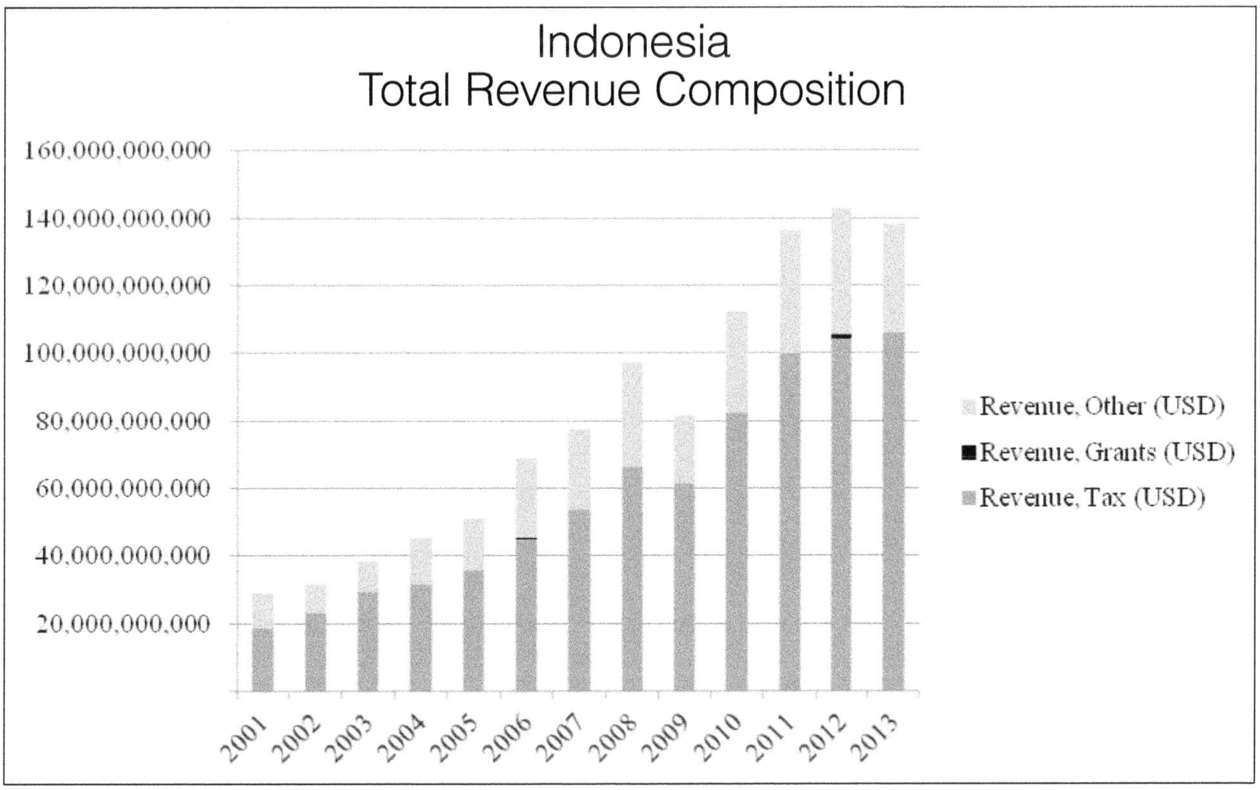
Indonesia
Total Revenue Composition
160,000,000,000
140,000,000,000
120,000,000,000
100,000,000,000
80,000,000,000
60,000,000,000
40,000,000,000
20,000,000,000
2001 2002 2003 2004 2005 2006 2007 2008 2009 2010 2011 2012 2013
Revenue, Other (USD)
Revenue, Grants (USD)
Revenue, Tax (USD)

Philippines[6]

Philippines	*Total Revenue (USD, millions)*	*Revenue, Tax Overall (USD, millions)*	*Revenue, Taxes of Income (USD, millions)*	*Revenue, Taxes on Goods and Services (USD, millions)*	*Revenue, Non-Tax (USD, millions)*
2001	11973	10295	4728	2212	1678
2002	11960	10414	4637	2359	1464
2003	12502	10740	4699	2601	1762
2004	13340	11421	5208	2650	1919
2005	15563	13399	6184	2989	2061
2006	19798	17476	7699	5255	2322
2007	23599	20910	9559	6124	2539
2008	27429	24478	11284	6944	2951
2009	29458	22052	9427	9258	7238
2010	33531	25747	10778	10977	7784
2011	39441	29581	13222	12998	9860
2012	45783	34275	15261	15261	11258
2013	50323	38354	16865	17681	11697

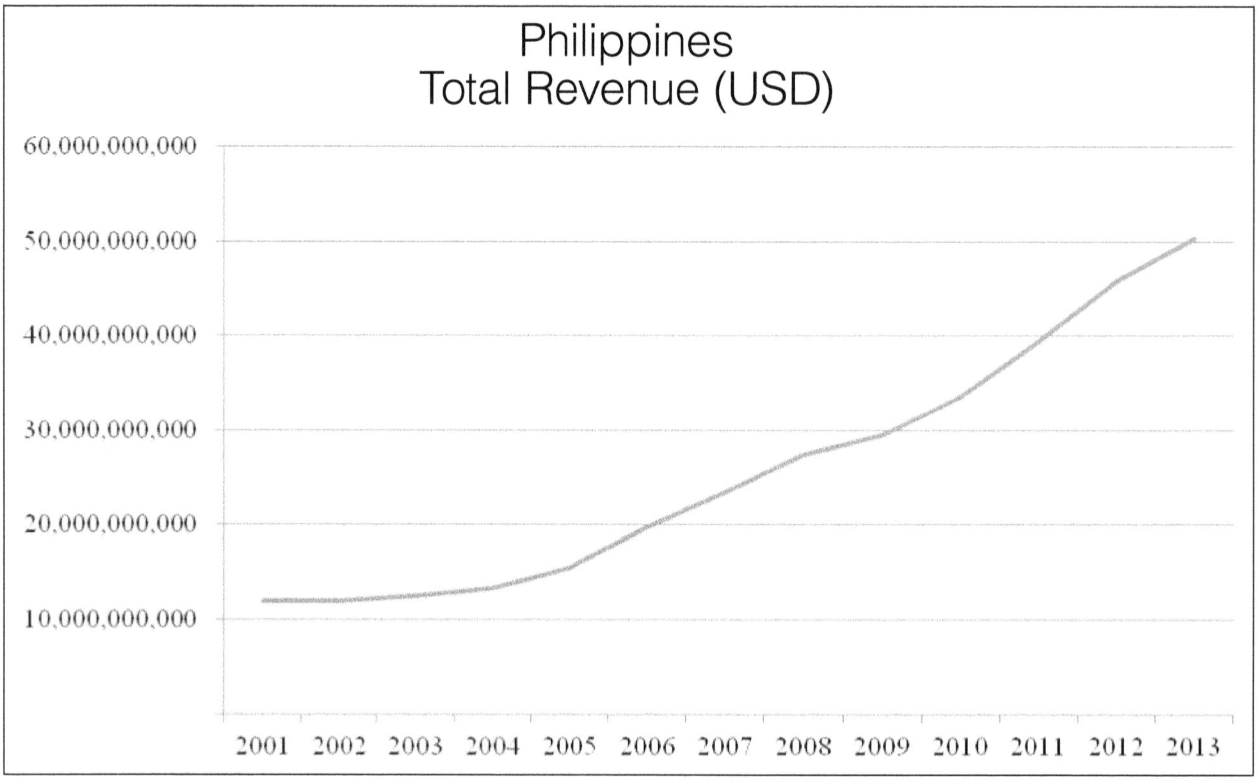

6. Metrics taken from IMF, "Philippines: 2013 Article IV Consultation," April 2013, http://www.imf.org/external/pubs/ft/scr/2013/cr13102.pdf. Final numbers were arrived at by multiplying metric as percent of GDP by GDP, as given in World Bank, "World Development Indicators: Philippines," http://databank.worldbank.org/data/views/variableSelection/selectvariables.aspx?source=world-development-indicators.

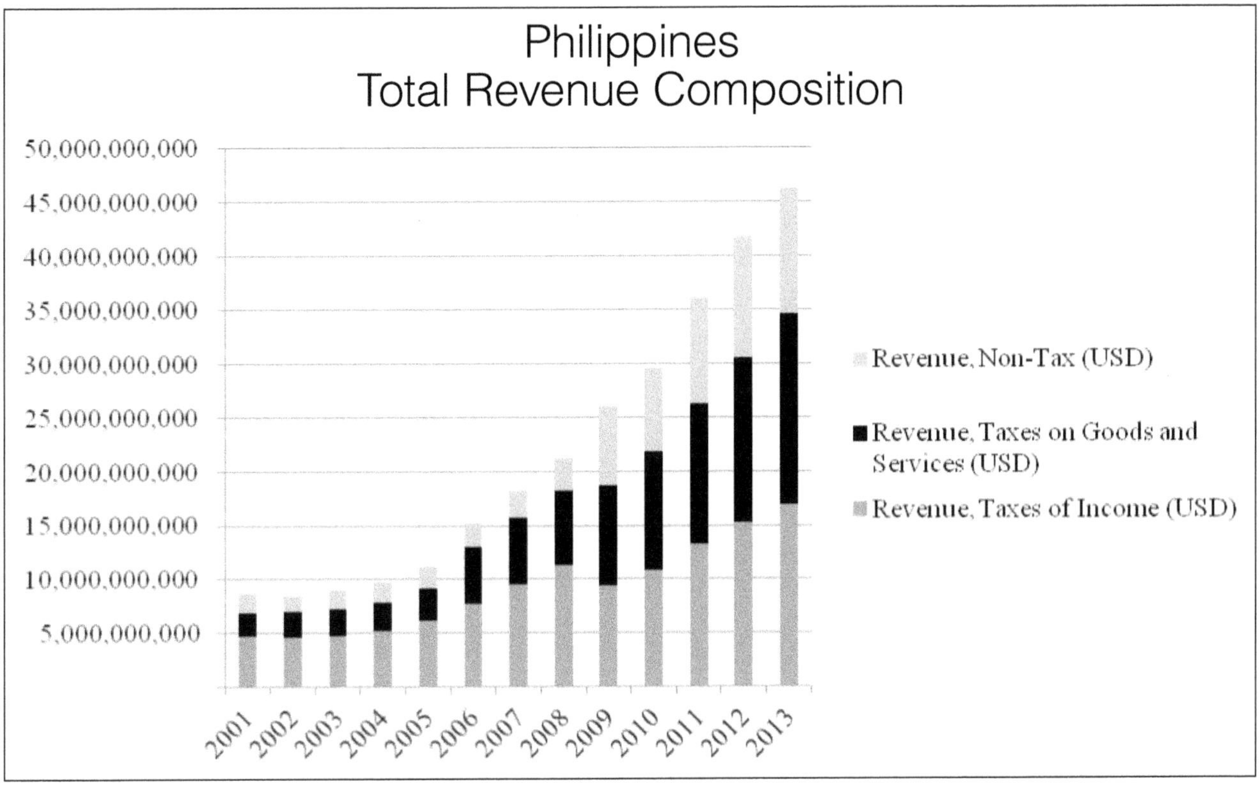

Vietnam[7]

Vietnam	*Total Revenue (USD, millions)*	*Revenue, Tax Overall (USD, millions)*	*Revenue, Oil (USD, millions)*	*Revenue, Grants (USD, millions)*	*Revenue, Other (USD, millions)*
2001	7623	4094	2612	141	776
2002	8614	4933	2580	152	949
2003	9868	5852	2734	128	1153
2004	11565	6722	3163	148	1532
2005	15676	13140	4553	288	NA
2006	19049	16128	5708	531	NA
2007	21366	17960	5187	310	NA
2008	28649	24287	5948	595	NA
2009	28942	23853	3923	530	636
2010	32229	27940	4058	348	NA
2011	37680	32801	5964	407	NA
2012	43474	39267	6077	312	NA
2013	47476	42848	6170	171	NA

7. Metrics taken from IMF, "Vietnam: 2014 Article IV Consultation," October 2014, http://www.imf.org/external/pubs/ft/scr/2014/cr14311.pdf. Final numbers were arrived at by multiplying metric as percent of GDP by GDP, as given in World Bank, "World Development Indicators: Vietnam," http://databank.worldbank.org/data/views/variableSelection/selectvariables.aspx?source=world-development-indicators.

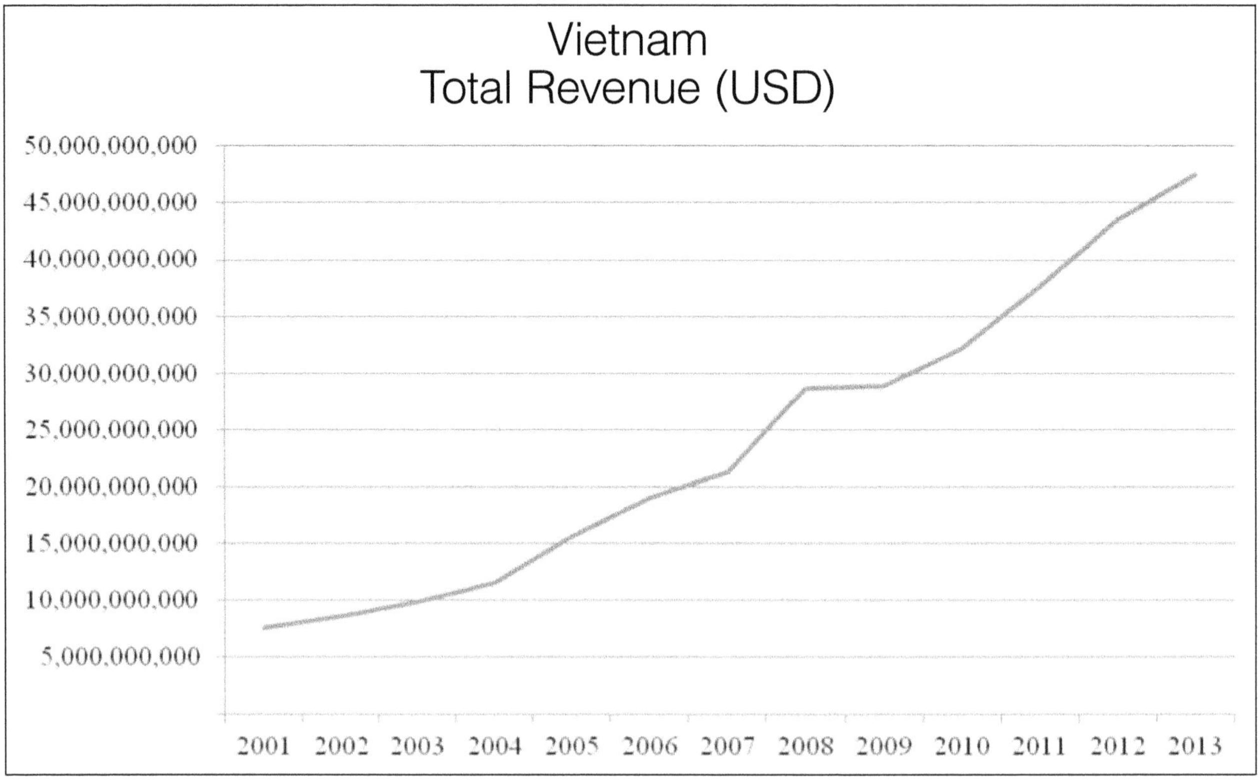
Vietnam
Total Revenue (USD)
50,000,000,000
45,000,000,000
40,000,000,000
35,000,000,000
30,000,000,000
25,000,000,000
20,000,000,000
15,000,000,000
10,000,000,000
5,000,000,000
2001 2002 2003 2004 2005 2006 2007 2008 2009 2010 2011 2012 2013

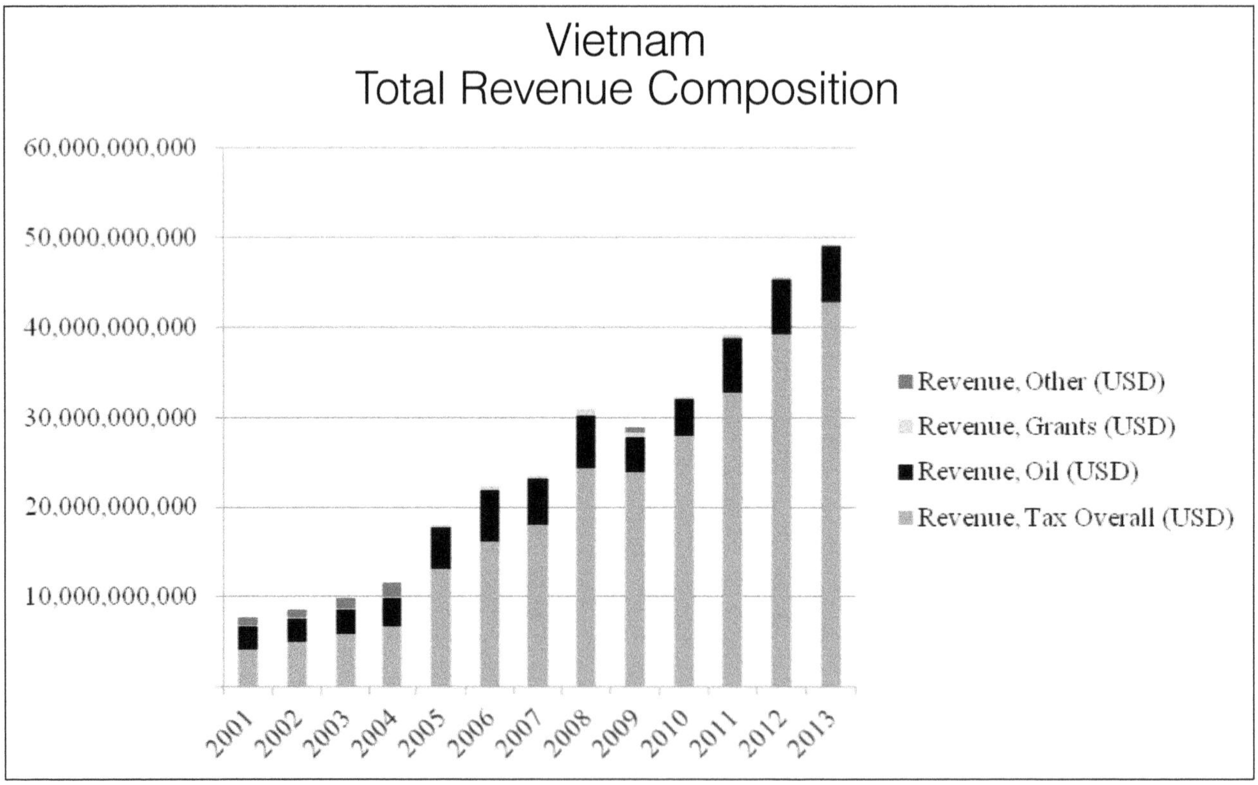
Vietnam
Total Revenue Composition
60,000,000,000
50,000,000,000
40,000,000,000
30,000,000,000
20,000,000,000
10,000,000,000
2001 2002 2003 2004 2005 2006 2007 2008 2009 2010 2011 2012 2013
Revenue, Other (USD)
Revenue, Grants (USD)
Revenue, Oil (USD)
Revenue, Tax Overall (USD)

Bangladesh[8]

Bangladesh	Total Revenue (USD, millions)	Revenue, Tax (USD, millions)	Revenue, Non-Tax (USD, millions)	Revenue, Other (USD, millions)
2001	4793	3618	1128	47
2002	4900	3948	951	NA
2003	5243	4257	986	NA
2004	5939	4864	1075	NA
2005	6329	5124	1206	NA
2006	6623	5262	1362	NA
2007	6978	5610	1368	NA
2008	8592	7001	1591	NA
2009	9651	7685	1698	268
2010	11541	9032	1907	602
2011	13317	11191	1902	224
2012	14968	12068	2321	580
2013	17790	14154	2987	649

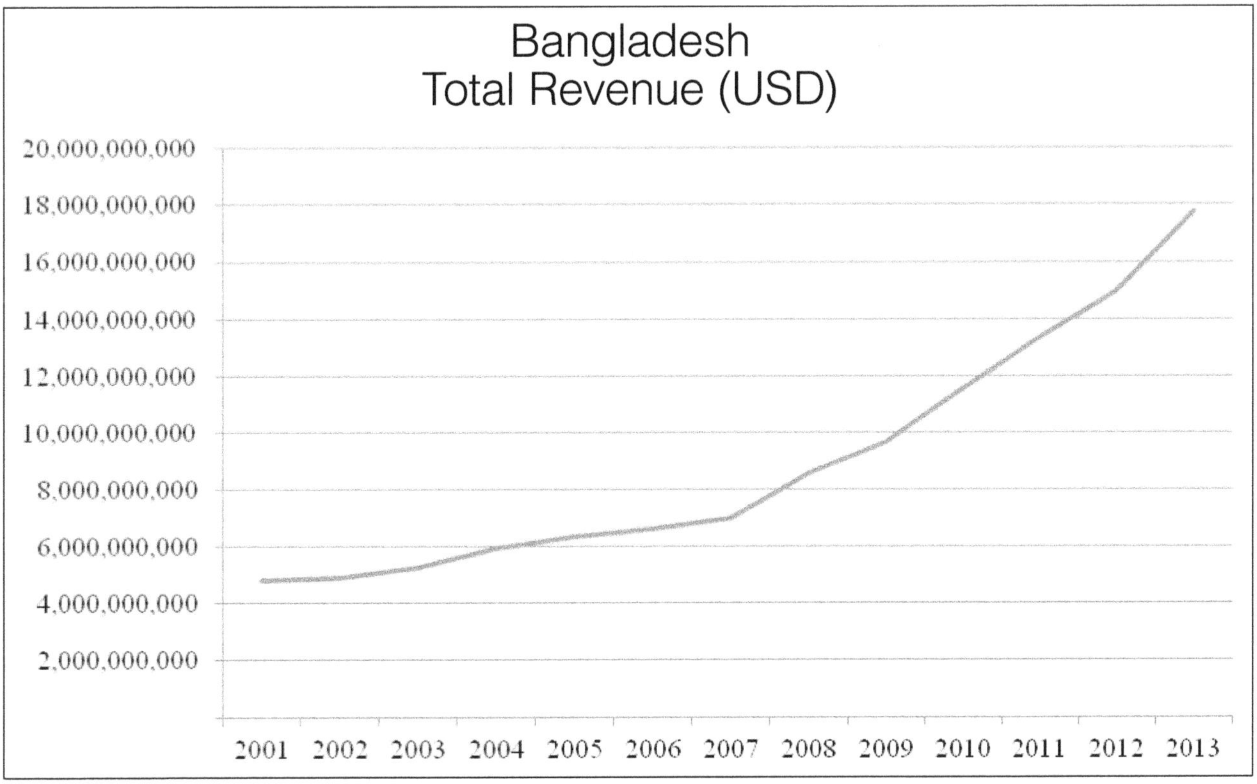

8. Metrics taken from IMF, "Bangladesh: 2011 Article IV Consultation," November 2011, http://www.imf.org/external/pubs/ft/scr/2011/cr11314.pdf. Final numbers were arrived at by multiplying metric as percent of GDP by GDP, as given in World Bank, "World Development Indicators: Bangladesh," http://databank.worldbank.org/data/views/variableSelection/selectvariables.aspx?source=world-development-indicators.

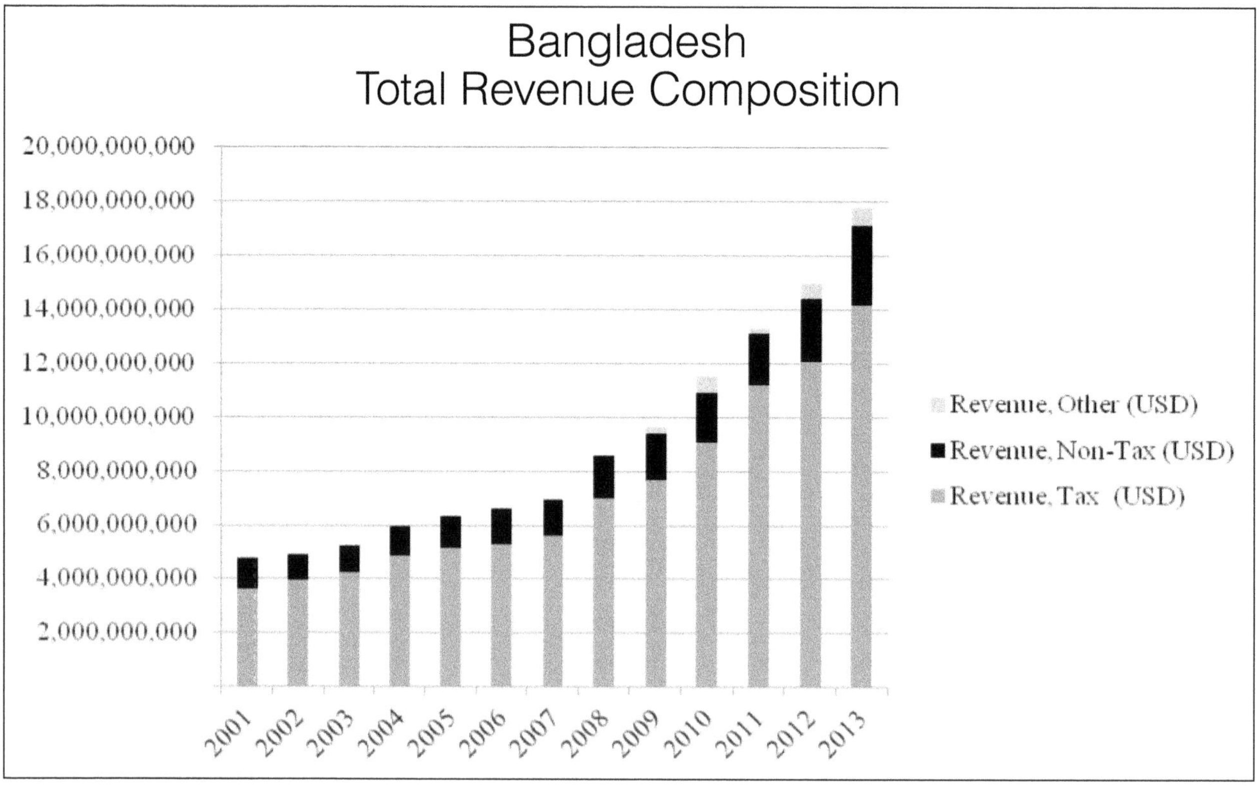

Ghana[9]

Ghana	*Total Revenue (USD, millions)*	*Revenue, Tax Overall (USD, millions)*	*Revenue, Direct Taxes (USD, millions)*	*Revenue, Indirect Taxes (USD, millions)*	*Revenue, Trade Taxes (USD, millions)*	*Revenue, Non-Tax (USD, millions)*	*Revenue, Grants (USD, millions)*
2001	1329	914	298	399	218	48	367
2002	1301	1079	351	475	253	31	191
2003	1946	1542	466	710	366	46	359
2004	2673	1927	586	915	426	133	568
2005	3123	2211	719	1041	451	343	558
2006	5592	4062	1265	1857	939	408	1102
2007	7130	4976	1659	2302	1015	644	1510
2008	7845	5677	2025	2482	1170	827	1341
2009	7794	5378	1896	2338	1169	831	1559
2010	9427	6757	2381	2928	1480	1062	1609
2011	13571	9575	4273	3482	1820	2453	1543
2012	7973	6595	3172	2296	1127	626	668
2013	8627	7333	3499	2588	1294	959	240

9. Metrics taken from IMF, "Ghana: 2014 Article IV Consultation," May 2014, http://www.imf.org/external/pubs/ft/scr/2014/cr14129.pdf. Final numbers were arrived at by multiplying metric as percent of GDP by GDP, as given in World Bank, "World Development Indicators: Ghana," http://databank.worldbank.org/data/views/variableSelection/selectvariables.aspx?source=world-development-indicators.

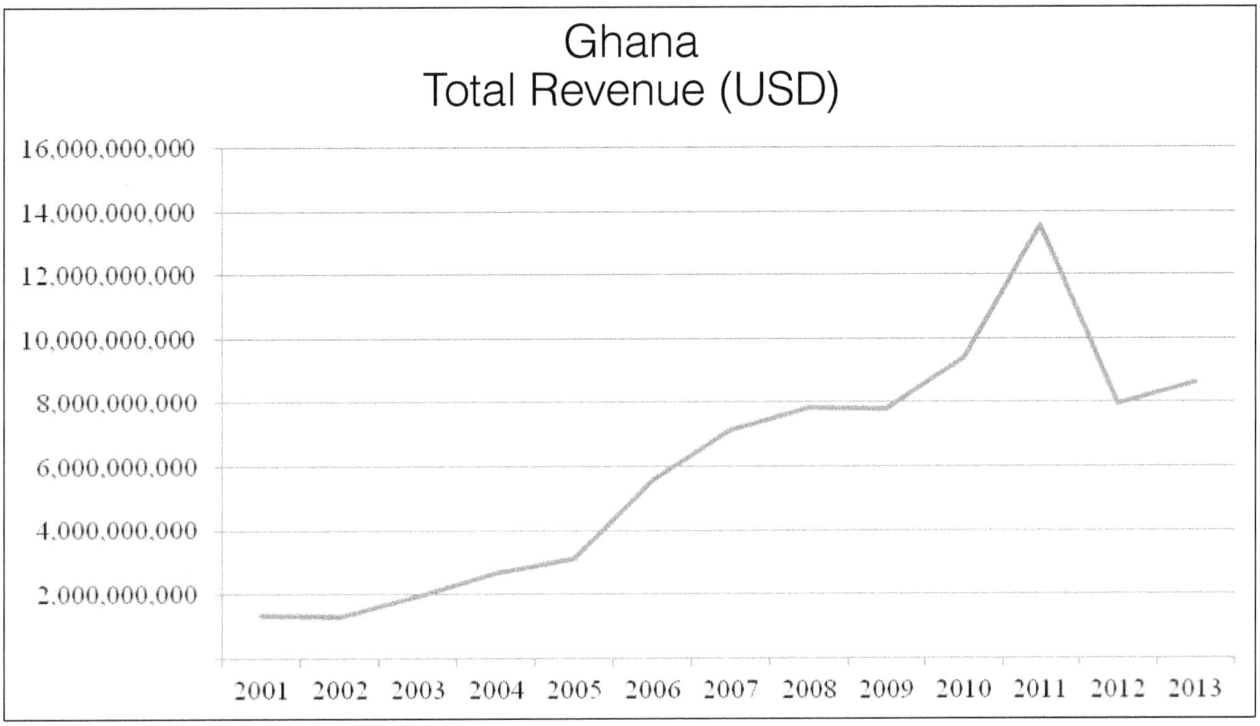
Ghana
Total Revenue (USD)
16,000,000,000
14,000,000,000
12,000,000,000
10,000,000,000
8,000,000,000
6,000,000,000
4,000,000,000
2,000,000,000
2001 2002 2003 2004 2005 2006 2007 2008 2009 2010 2011 2012 2013

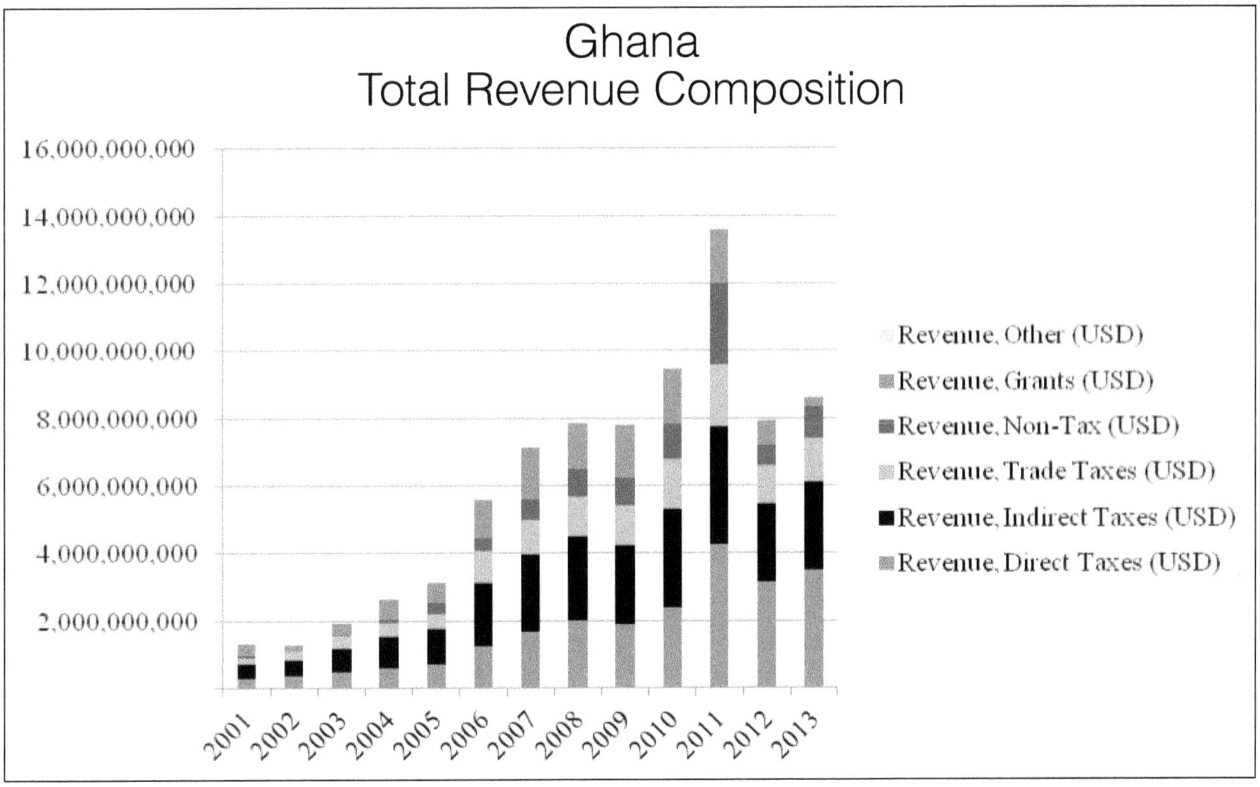
Ghana
Total Revenue Composition
16,000,000,000
14,000,000,000
12,000,000,000
10,000,000,000
8,000,000,000
6,000,000,000
4,000,000,000
2,000,000,000
2001 2002 2003 2004 2005 2006 2007 2008 2009 2010 2011 2012 2013
Revenue, Other (USD)
Revenue, Grants (USD)
Revenue, Non-Tax (USD)
Revenue, Trade Taxes (USD)
Revenue, Indirect Taxes (USD)
Revenue, Direct Taxes (USD)

Tanzania[10]

Tanzania	*Total Revenue (USD, millions)*	*Revenue, Tax Overall (USD, millions)*	*Revenue, Income Taxes (USD, millions)*	*Revenue, VAT (USD, millions)*	*Revenue, Non-Tax (USD, millions)*
2001	1256	1132	280	426	125
2002	1307	1189	292	454	119
2003	1446	1317	315	513	128
2004	1731	1590	423	628	141
2005	1768	1626	467	665	156
2006	2021	1863	530	616	158
2007	2675	2473	723	774	202
2008	3356	3169	953	953	186
2009	3376	3120	940	983	256
2010	3758	3483	1100	1008	298
2011	4202	3772	1313	1146	430
2012	5113	4633	1667	1356	480
2013	6612	5947	2027	1628	665

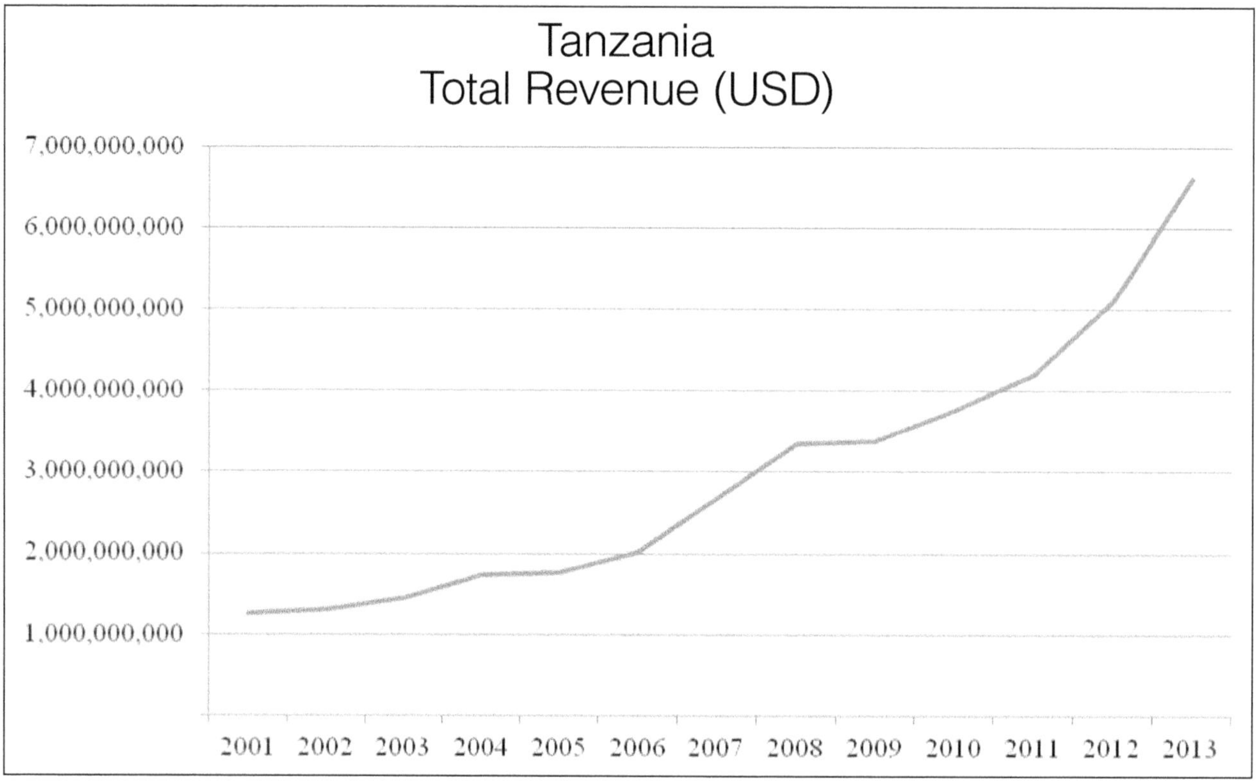

10. Metrics taken from IMF, "United Republic of Tanzania: 2014 Article IV Consultation," May 2014, http://www.imf.org/external/pubs/ft/scr/2014/cr14120.pdf. Final numbers were arrived at by multiplying metric as percent of GDP by GDP, as given in World Bank, "World Development Indicators: Tanzania," http://databank.worldbank.org/data/views/variableSelection/selectvariables.aspx?source=world-development-indicators.

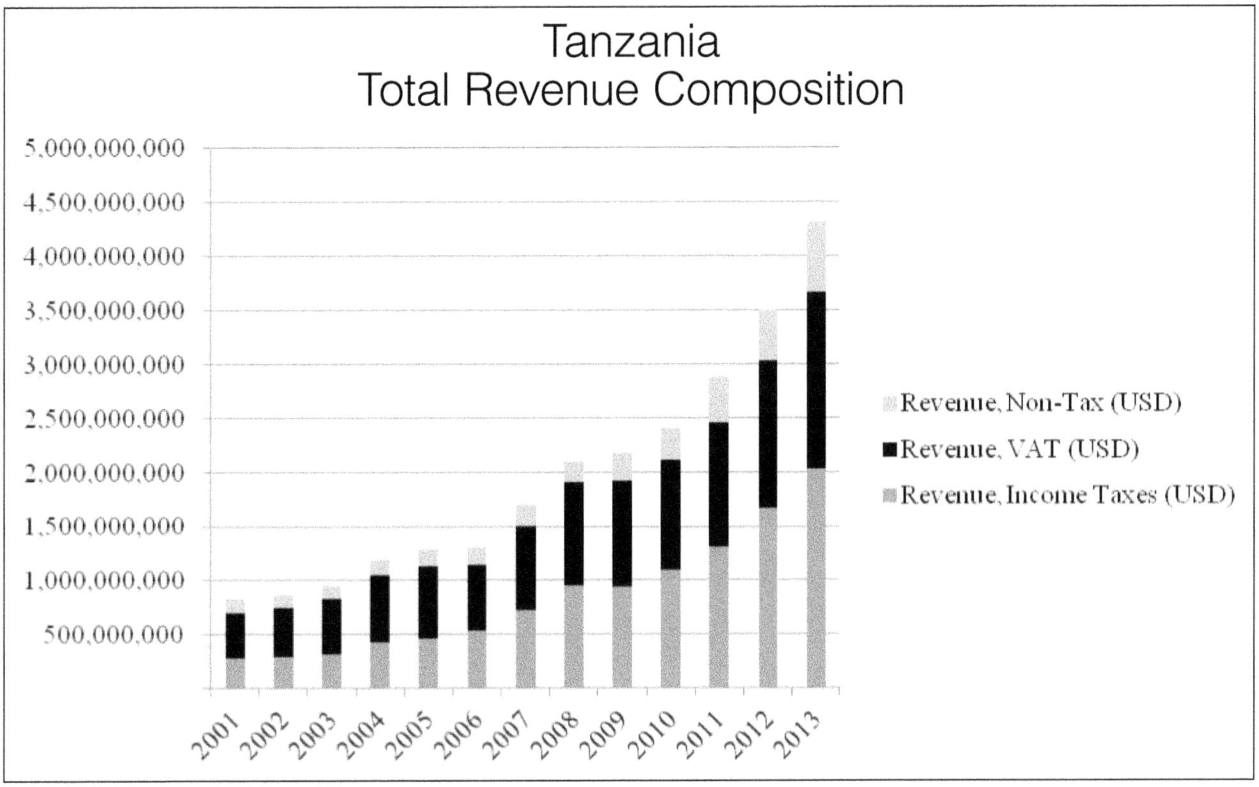

Zambia[11]

Zambia	*Total Revenue (USD, millions)*	*Revenue, Tax Overall (USD, millions)*	*Revenue, Income Taxes (USD, millions)*	*Revenue, VAT (USD, millions)*	*Revenue, Grants (USD, millions)*	*Revenue, Other (USD, millions)*
2001	910	683	274	230	212	15
2002	972	649	282	186	308	15
2003	1081	751	343	221	304	26
2004	1295	952	424	288	299	44
2005	1651	1220	546	359	402	29
2006	4591	1723	803	492	2783	86
2007	2655	2043	958	554	531	81
2008	3367	2577	1244	586	600	190
2009	2420	1870	960	487	371	179
2010	3173	2655	1441	664	291	227
2011	4320	3706	2189	826	307	307
2012	4305	3419	1689	927	350	536
2013	5081	3984	2059	1052	425	672

11. Metrics taken from IMF, "Zambia: 2012 Article IV Consultation," July 2012, http://www.imf.org/external/pubs/ft/scr/2012/cr12200.pdf. Final numbers were arrived at by multiplying metric as percent of GDP by GDP, as given in World Bank, "World Development Indicators: Zambia," http://databank.worldbank.org/data/views/variableSelection/selectvariables.aspx?source=world-development-indicators.

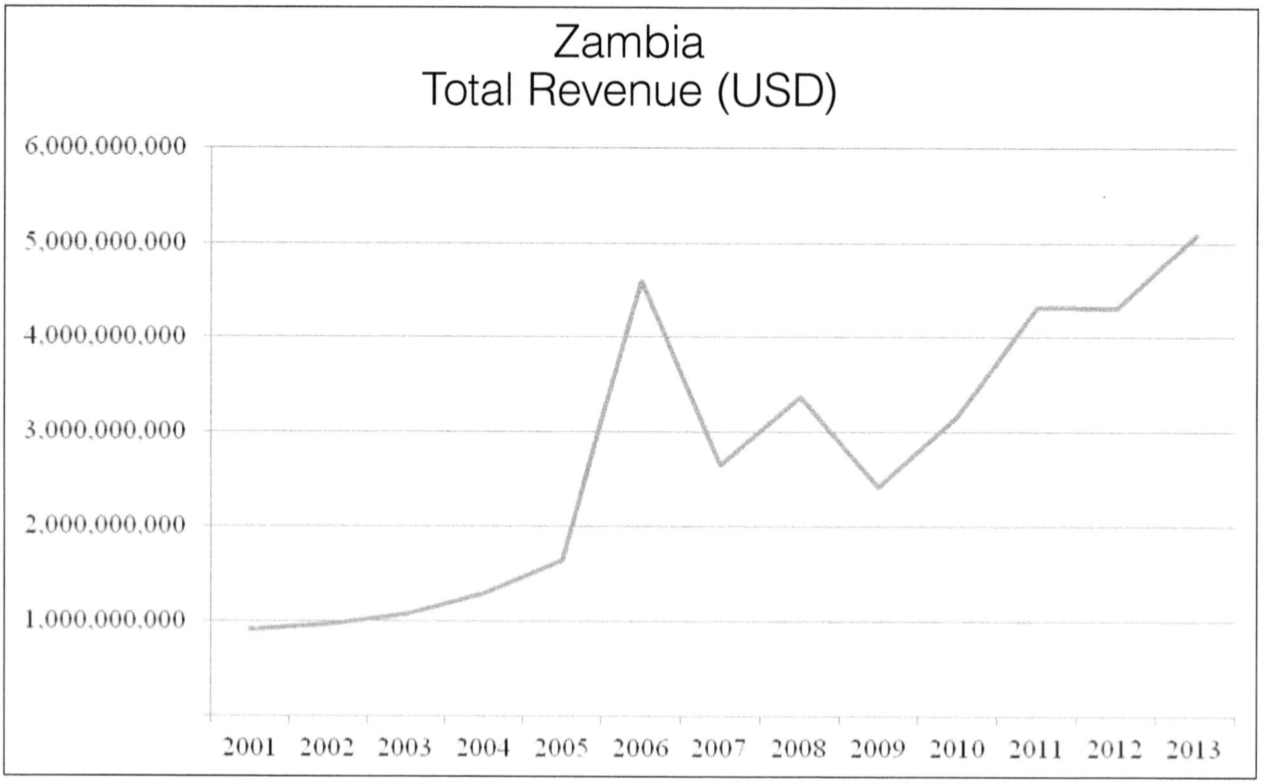
Zambia
Total Revenue (USD)
6,000,000,000
5,000,000,000
4,000,000,000
3,000,000,000
2,000,000,000
1,000,000,000
2001
2002
2003
2004
2005
2006
2007
2008
2009
2010
2011
2012
2013

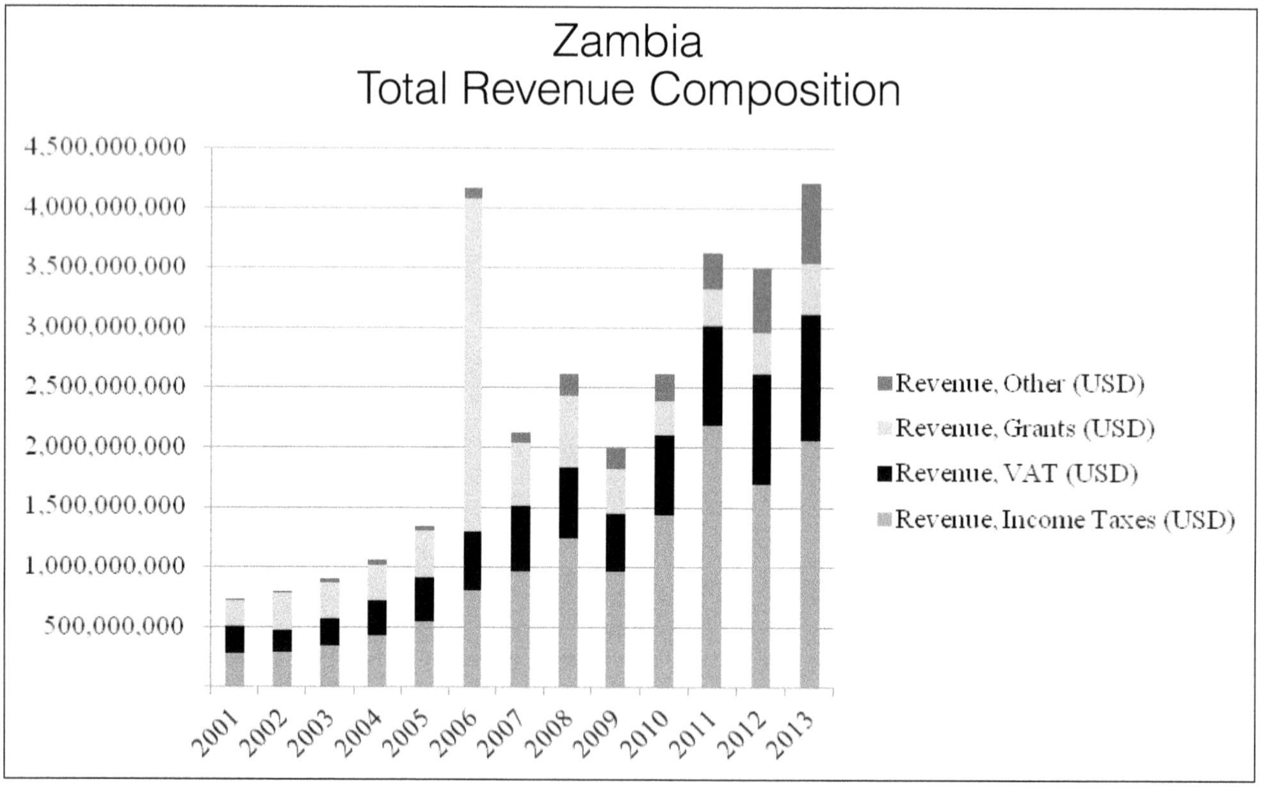
Zambia
Total Revenue Composition
4,500,000,000
4,000,000,000
3,500,000,000
3,000,000,000
2,500,000,000
2,000,000,000
1,500,000,000
1,000,000,000
500,000,000
2001
2002
2003
2004
2005
2006
2007
2008
2009
2010
2011
2012
2013
Revenue, Other (USD)
Revenue, Grants (USD)
Revenue, VAT (USD)
Revenue, Income Taxes (USD)

Senegal[12]

Senegal	Total Revenue (USD, millions)	Revenue, Tax Overall (USD, millions)	Revenue, Non-Tax (USD, millions)	Revenue, Grants (USD, millions)	Revenue, Other (USD, millions)
2001	971	844	39	88	NA
2002	1115	965	53	96	NA
2003	1379	1173	75	137	NA
2004	1654	1414	72	169	NA
2005	1916	1680	78	157	NA
2006	2003	1778	75	140	9
2007	2663	2268	102	293	NA
2008	2918	2450	147	321	NA
2009	2832	2409	77	346	NA
2010	2832	2444	91	297	NA
2011	3235	2729	101	318	87
2012	3287	2739	98	379	70
2013	3530	2909	151	394	76

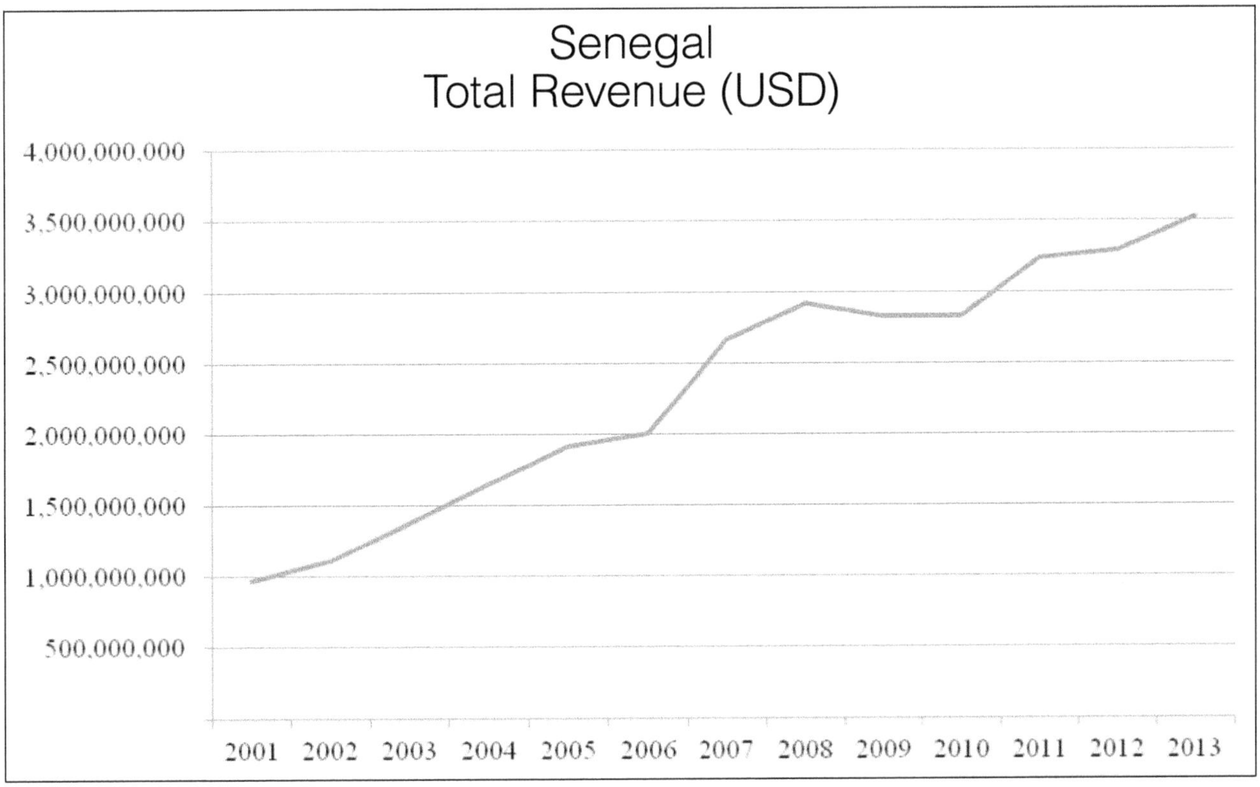

12. Metrics taken from IMF, "Senegal: Staff Report for the 2012 Article IV Consultation," November 2012, http://www.imf.org/external/pubs/ft/scr/2012/cr12337.pdf. Final numbers were arrived at by multiplying metric as percent of GDP by GDP, as given in World Bank, "World Development Indicators: Senegal," http://databank.worldbank.org/data/views/variableSelection/selectvariables.aspx?source=world-development-indicators.

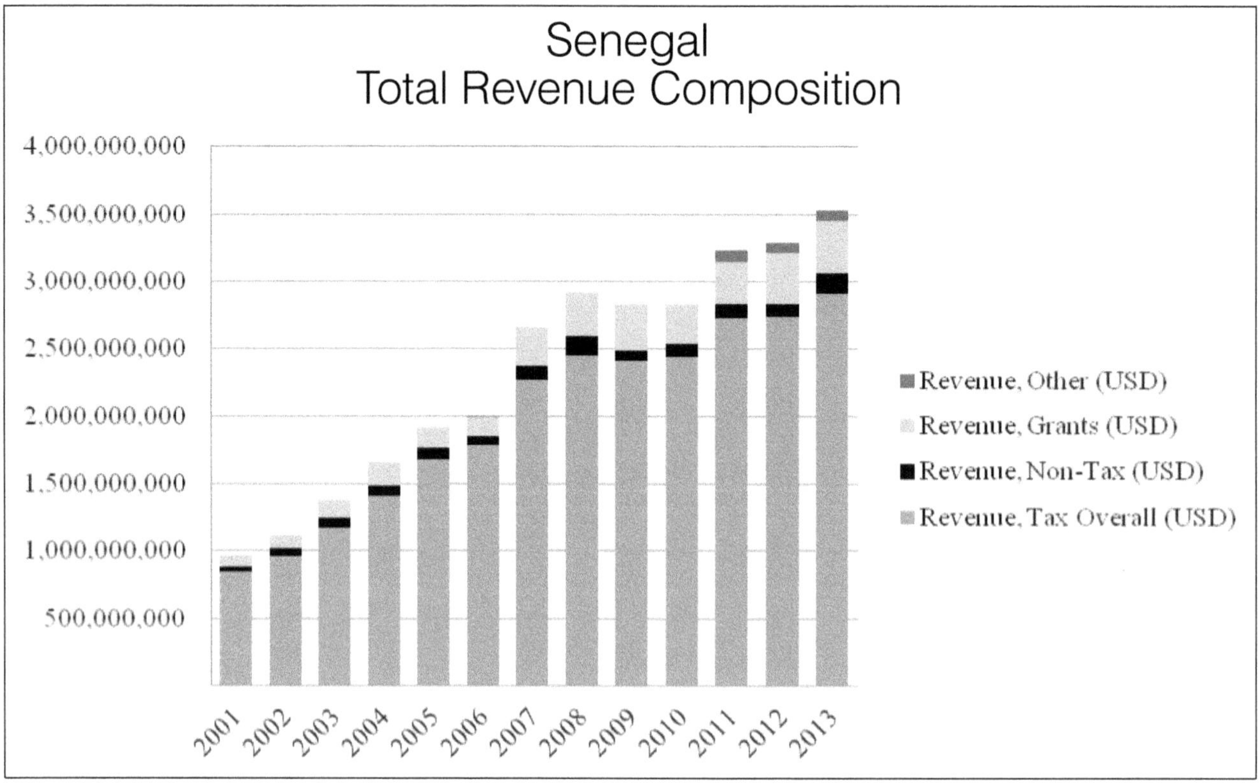

Regional Tax Revenue Comparisons

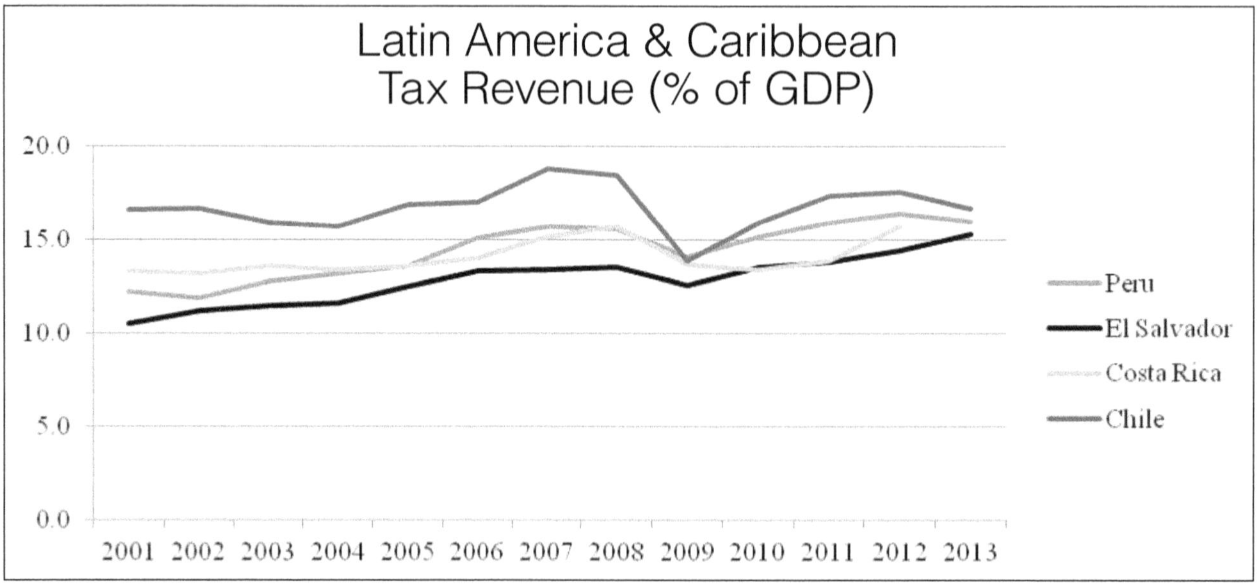

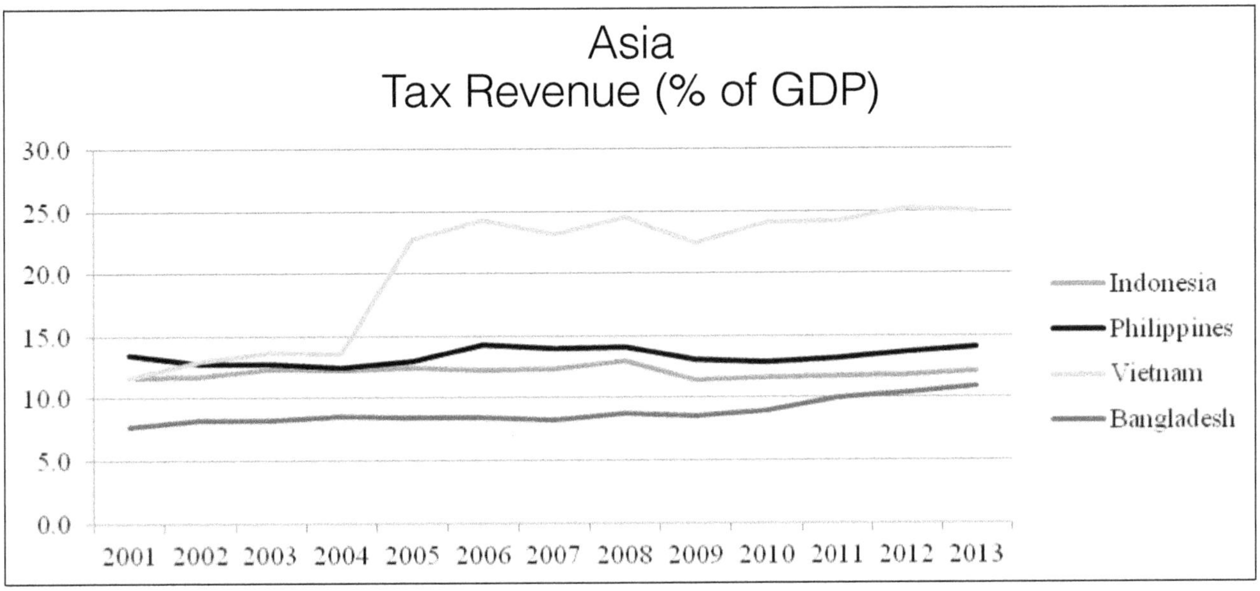
Asia
Tax Revenue (% of GDP)
30.0
25.0
20.0
15.0
10.0
5.0
0.0
2001 2002 2003 2004 2005 2006 2007 2008 2009 2010 2011 2012 2013
Indonesia
Philippines
Vietnam
Bangladesh

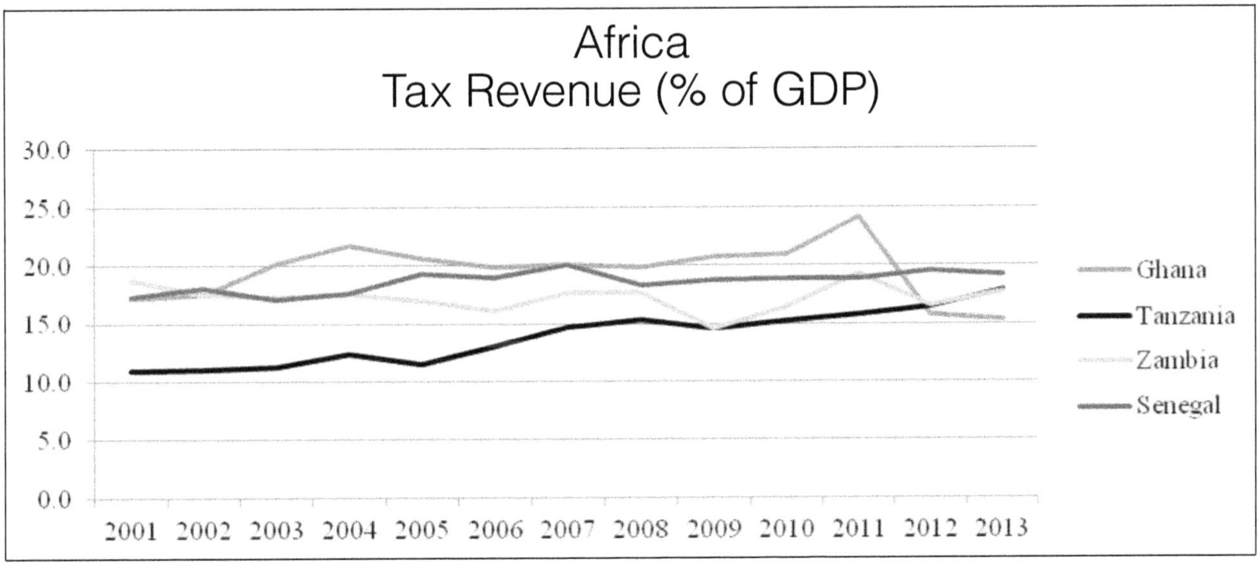
Africa
Tax Revenue (% of GDP)
30.0
25.0
20.0
15.0
10.0
5.0
0.0
2001 2002 2003 2004 2005 2006 2007 2008 2009 2010 2011 2012 2013
Ghana
Tanzania
Zambia
Senegal

About the Project Director and Authors

Daniel F. Runde is director of the Project on U.S. Leadership in Development and holds the William A. Schreyer Chair in Global Analysis at CSIS. He focuses on private enterprise development, the role of private actors in development (philanthropy, business, diasporas, and others), and the role of "emerging donors" (e.g., members of the G20). Previously, Mr. Runde was head of the Foundations Unit for the Department of Partnerships and Advisory Service Operations at the International Finance Corporation (IFC), the private-sector arm of the World Bank Group, where he successfully positioned IFC as a partner of choice for private and corporate philanthropy. He was also responsible for leading IFC's relations with senior policymakers throughout the U.S. government. From 2005 to 2007, he was director of the Office of Global Development Alliances (GDA) at the U.S. Agency for International Development (USAID), and he led the GDA partnership initiative by providing training, networks, staff, funds, and advice to establish and strengthen alliances. His efforts leveraged $4.8 billion through 100 direct alliances and 300 others through training and technical assistance.

Earlier in his career, Mr. Runde worked for both CitiBank and BankBoston in Buenos Aires, Argentina. He started his career with Alex. Brown & Sons, Inc., in Baltimore. He was named in September 2010 as one of "40 under 40 in International Development in Washington" by the Devex Group. He is actively involved in the philanthropic sector as a member of committees for the Global Philanthropy Forum and the Committee Encouraging Corporate Philanthropy. He is a board member of the Society for International Development, the Peter C. Alderman Foundation, the Alliance for the Family, and the Advisory Boards of the UN Development Program's Growing Inclusive Markets Initiative. He has written and spoken extensively on public-private partnership issues at global conferences and symposia. Mr. Runde received an M.P.P from the Kennedy School of Government at Harvard University and a B.A., cum laude, from Dartmouth College.

Conor M. Savoy is deputy director and fellow with the Project on U.S. Leadership in Development (USLD) at CSIS. He joined CSIS in September 2011 as assistant director of USLD. At CSIS, he focuses on implementing and guiding USLD's research agenda. He has contributed to several reports, commentaries, and critical questions. He is the coauthor of *The Ecosystem of U.S. International Development Assistance: A Development and Foreign Policy Strategic Asset* (CSIS, October 2012) and *U.S.-China Parallel Development Assistance Goals: Building on Common Interests* (CSIS, March 2012). Prior to this, he worked in energy consulting and as a research associate at the Council on Foreign Relations (CFR) in Washington, D.C. At CFR, he focused on broad issues impacting U.S. grand strategy, the effect of emerging nations on U.S. foreign policy, as well as U.S.-Russia relations and NATO. In May 2010, he was selected as a fellow for the Manfred Worner Seminar. Mr. Savoy holds a B.A. with honors in history from George Washington University and an M.A. in international relations from Boston University.

Christina M. Perkins is program manager and research assistant with the Project on U.S. Leadership in Development at CSIS, where she supports research, logistics, and outreach efforts. Prior to joining CSIS, she served as local program director with Yspaniola in the Dominican Republic, where she managed youth education and community development programs. She has also worked in communications with the Atlas Economic Research Foundation and Relief International. Ms. Perkins holds a B.A. in international development studies with a minor in Spanish from the University of California at Los Angeles.

www.ingramcontent.com/pod-product-compliance
Ingram Content Group UK Ltd.
Pitfield, Milton Keynes, MK11 3LW, UK
UKHW051418150926
475561UK00005B/238

9 781442 24